EVERYDAY LIFE
IN ROMAN AND
ANGLO-SAXON TIMES

EVERYDAY LIFE
IN ROMAN AND
ANGLO-SAXON TIMES

Including
VIKING AND NORMAN TIMES

By
MARJORIE & C. H. B. QUENNELL

LONDON: B. T. BATSFORD LTD
NEW YORK: G. P. PUTNAM'S SONS

"*Everyday Life in Roman Britain*"
Fifth Impression, 1957
"*Everyday Life in Anglo-Saxon, Viking and
Norman Times*"
Fourth edition, 1955
First published, revised in one volume, 1959
Fifth impression 1968

PRINTED AND BOUND IN GREAT BRITAIN BY JARROLD AND SONS LTD
LONDON AND NORWICH
FOR THE PUBLISHERS
B. T. BATSFORD LTD, 4 FITZHARDINGE STREET, PORTMAN SQUARE, LONDON, W.1
G. P. PUTNAM'S SONS, 200 MADISON AVENUE, NEW YORK, N.Y. 10016

PREFACE

THE boys and girls for whom we write, may have read the *Life of Agricola*, by Tacitus, and so know the fine Epilogue with which it closes.

"And I would lay this charge on his daughter and his wife—so to reverence the memory of their father, and husband, that they revolve within them all that he said and did, and to cherish the form and the fashion of his soul, rather than of his body; it is not that I would forbid the making of statues, shaped in marble or bronze, but that as the human face, so is its copy—futile and perishing, while the form of the mind is eternal, to be expressed, not through the alien medium of art and its material, but severally by each man in the fashion of his own life."

Tacitus was writing of the character of his father-in-law, Agricola, and gave us at the same time a hint of what we should look for in history. If only the spirit is eternal, it is very obvious that we must make diligent search for the principles which have animated men in the past and helped them to fashion their souls. To search for motive is apt to be an arid study; political history, and its recital of how statesmen have bested their friends, and ruined their enemies, makes dull reading, unless it is inspired. There remains the possibility of judging men by their works. This was the only method in the Prehistoric periods, and it is on the whole a very safe one.

In dealing with Roman history we shall find the historians divided into two schools, one of which will glorify the Republic, and think the Empire was all decline and fall; the other will thrill at the Augustan Age. It is safe to predict, that to whichever school we attach ourselves, or even if we form an opinion of our own, we shall leave off with a feeling of great respect for the Roman sense of law and order.

When a nation not only makes laws, but agrees to keep them, it is a sign of a very advanced state of civilization. With this Roman power of administration, we shall note great developments in the art of town-planning, building, and civil

5

engineering. Yet all this wonderful structure came tumbling down, because the fashion of the Roman soul was too material.

The period dealt with in this book is vital to us because the introduction of Christianity into Great Britain dates from the Roman Occupation, and conflicted in a thousand ways with the Roman conception of life and living.

The Roman was tolerant. Caesar writing of the gods of the Gauls, said they were much the same as other peoples, and the Romans, as a proud and conquering race, were not alarmed at the preaching of the disciples of an obscure Jew who had been crucified in Palestine. They persecuted the Christians, not so much for saying that man was made in the image of God, but for political rather than for religious reasons. It is almost impossible for us, with centuries of Christian teaching behind us, to estimate the first effect of the teaching of the Apostles. We know the teaching, even if we neglect it, but to have heard the Sermon on the Mount, as a Roman, for the first time, must have been an extraordinary experience. If he believed the teaching, then his confidence as a Roman was gone, because Christianity was the negation of the Roman way of living, and contributed to its downfall.

Ambrose, Bishop of Milan, made Theodosius the Emperor, in A.D. 390, divest himself of the purple and do public penance for a massacre carried out by his troops. Power had passed to the Church.

In the wide region of Statecraft, we can watch the efforts of man to govern himself. The hill forts we saw in Vol. I could only have been formed under some system of tribal government, and in the historic period, we find Kings and Empires, Tyrannies, Democracies, and Republics, tried one after the other, in man's search for the proper method of living.

From the time of the Roman Occupation, so far as Europe was concerned, Christianity was destined to become the great force by which men set the "fashion of their souls"; it civilized men again after the dark ages following on the fall of Rome, and inspired the Crusades. Churches were planned to be cruciform, and the figure of Christ was cut in stone, and glowed in the jewelled glass of a thousand windows.

It follows, then, that we are in sympathy with all the people, who, since A.D. was used in the calendar, have been confronted with similar problems of life and death, of joy and sorrow, and of how life is to be made sweet and wholesome.

The statesman reads history to find how man can be helped to this end, and his trouble is the same as ours, how to make the dry bones live. There are times of enlightenment.

Our readers will sometimes have seen visions, and dreamed dreams. There are days, or better still nights, when the tired body is sloughed off, and the brain rides untrammelled, and we understand the meaning of things. The time curtains roll back a little on one side, and we have a walking part in the scene; we may not speak to the principal actors, but we are close to them; we catch the fragrance of Wolsey's orange as he passes along, and the figures of history become instead of names, men and women of flesh and blood.

We begin to form certain opinions of our own; one period may seem brave and cheerful, another dark and gloomy. For this reason, perhaps, history has been very much concerned with the doings of great men; even the terrible villains serve the useful purpose of shadow in the picture, and throw into relief the brightness of the heroes. If these have been rather dispensers of Death, than saviours of life, like Pasteur, then it is our own fault for having worshipped at the wrong shrine. This question of the atmosphere of history is worth testing by our own experience; this may be limited, but we can try to find out why a particular school, or form, or term, or individual, will leave an impression on our minds. The importance of history, or tradition, is that it gives us a standard against which we can measure our own effort, and as history is concerned just as much with work as war, so work is concerned with the doings of untold myriads of individuals much the same as ourselves.

MARJORIE and C. H. B. QUENNELL

7

CONTENTS

ACKNOWLEDGMENT

The Authors and Publishers wish to thank the following for permission to reproduce the illustrations appearing in this book:

The British Council, for fig. 84.

The Trustees of the British Museum, for figs. 97–9, 121–3 and 132.

Mrs. D. Holland, for fig. 99.

Trinity College, Dublin, for fig. 133.

The Trustees of the Victoria and Albert Museum, for fig. 85.

Fig. 83 is a Royal Air Force official photograph, and is Crown copyright reserved; fig. 120 is from *Die Reliefs der Traians-Saule* by C. Cichorius, Berlin, 1896–1900; fig. 109 from *Medieval Archaeology* (Journal of the Society for Medieval Archaeology), Volume I, 1957; and fig. 124 from *Late Saxon and Viking Art* T. D. Kendrick (Methuen & Co. Ltd.).

LIST OF ILLUSTRATIONS

The numerals in parentheses in the text refer to the
figure numbers of the illustrations

11

LIST OF ILLUSTRATIONS

LIST OF ILLUSTRATIONS

13

LIST OF ILLUSTRATIONS

BIBLIOGRAPHY

G. M. BOUMPHREY: *Along the Roman Roads.* (1935.)

CAESAR: *The Conquest of Gaul.* (Penguin Books, 1951.)

M. P. CHARLESWORTH: *The Lost Province.* (Cardiff, 1949.)

R. G. COLLINGWOOD: *The Archaeology of Roman Britain.* (Methuen, 1930.)

R. G. COLLINGWOOD and J. N. L. MYERS. *Roman Britain and the English Settlements.* (Oxford, 1945.)

J. CURLE: *A Roman Frontier Post: Newstead.* (1911.)

I. D. MARGARY: *Roman Roads in Britain.* (Phœnix House, Vol I, 1955; Vol II, 1957).

F. HAVERFIELD: *The Romanization of Roman Britain.* (Oxford, 1923.)

F. HAVERFIELD and G. MACDONALD: *The Roman Occupation of Britain.* (Oxford, 1924.)

G. MACDONALD: *The Roman Wall in Scotland.* (Oxford, 1934.)

R. W. MOORE: *The Romans in Britain.* A selection of Latin Texts. (Methuen, 1938.)

IAN RICHMOND: *Roman Britain.* (Collins, 1947.)

IAN RICHMOND: *Roman Britain.* (Penguin Books, 1955.)

A. L. F. RIVET: *Town and Country in Roman Britain.* (Hutchinson, 1957.)

TACITUS: *On Great Britain and Germany.* (Penguin Books, 1948.)

ORDNANCE SURVEY: *Map of Roman Britain.* With very good Lists and Introduction. (3rd edition, 1956.)

P. HUNTER BLAIR: *Anglo-Saxon England.* (Cambridge, 1956.)

GAVIN BONE: *Anglo-Saxon Poetry.* (Oxford, 1944.)

G. BALDWIN BROWN: *The Arts in Early England.* Six volumes. (John Murray, 1925.)

H. M. CHADWICK: *The Heroic Age.* (Cambridge, 1912.)

H. M. and N. K. CHADWICK: *The Growth of Literature.* (Cambridge, 1932.)

A. W. CLAPHAM: *English Romanesque Architecture before the Conquest.* (Oxford, 1930.)

R. G. COLLINGWOOD and J. N. L. MYERS: *Roman Britain and the English Settlements.* (Oxford, 1945.)

G. W. DASENT: *The Story of Burnt Njal.* (Dent, Everyman Library), N.D.

ELEANOR DUCKETT: *Anglo-Saxon Saints and Scholars.* (Macmillan, 1947.)

J. R. CLARK HALL: *Beowulf.* (Cambridge, 1914.)

G. A. HIGHT: *The Saga of Grettir the Strong.* (Dent, Everyman Library, 1929.)

R. H. HODGKIN: *History of the Anglo-Saxons.* (Cambridge, 1935.)

RONALD JESSUP: *Anglo-Saxon Jewellery.* (Faber, 1950.)

16

BIBLIOGRAPHY

T. D. KENDRICK: *Anglo-Saxon Art*. (Methuen, 1938.)

T. D. KENDRICK: *A History of the Vikings*. (Methuen, 1930.)

T. D. KENDRICK: *Late Saxon and Viking Art*. (Methuen, 1949.)

E. T. LEEDS: *Early Anglo-Saxon Art and Archaeology*. (Oxford, 1936.)

ERLING MONSEN: *Heimskringla, or the lives of the Norse Kings*. (Heffer, 1931.)

D. D. C. POCHIN MOULD: *Scotland of the Saints*. (Batsford, 1952.)

D. D. C. POCHIN MOULD: *Ireland of the Saints*. (Batsford, 1953.)

F. M. STENTON: *Anglo-Saxon England*. (Oxford, 1943.)

SUTTON HOO SHIP BURIAL. (British Museum, 1947.)

D. TALBOT RICE: *English Art*, 871–1110. (Oxford, 1952.)

A. H. THOMPSON: *Bede*. (Oxford, 1935.)

D. M. WILSON, *The Anglo-Saxons*. (Thames and Hudson, 1960.)

17

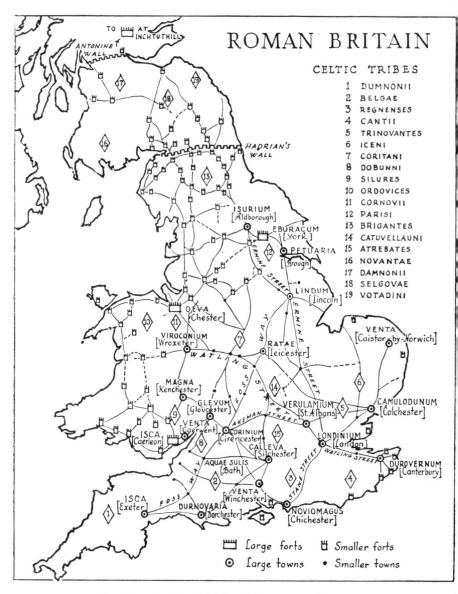

ROMAN BRITAIN

CELTIC TRIBES

1 DUMNONII
2 BELGAE
3 REGNENSES
4 CANTII
5 TRINOVANTES
6 ICENI
7 CORITANI
8 DOBUNNI
9 SILURES
10 ORDOVICES
11 CORNOVII
12 PARISI
13 BRIGANTES
14 CATUVELLAUNI
15 ATREBATES
16 NOVANTAE
17 DAMNONII
18 SELGOVAE
19 VOTADINI

TO AT INCHTUTHILL

ANTONINE WALL

HADRIAN'S WALL

ISURIUM [Aldborough]

EBURACUM [York]

PETUARIA [Brough]

LINDUM [Lincoln]

DEVA [Chester]

VIROCONIUM [Wroxeter]

VENTA [Caistor-by-Norwich]

RATAE [Leicester]

WATLING

MAGNA [Kenchester]

VERULAMIUM [St. Albans]

CAMULODUNUM [Colchester]

GLEVUM [Gloucester]

ISCA [Caerleon]

VENTA [Caerwent]

CORINIUM [Cirencester]

AKEMAN STREET

CALLEVA [Silchester]

LONDINIUM [London]

WATLING STREET

DUROVERNUM [Canterbury]

AQUAE SULIS [Bath]

VENTA [Winchester]

ISCA [Exeter]

FOSS

DURNOVARIA [Dorchester]

NOVIOMAGUS [Chichester]

ERMINE STREET

STANE STREET

☖ Large forts   ♜ Smaller forts
⊙ Large towns   • Smaller towns

1   Map showing British and Roman road systems

Chapter 1

THE HERITAGE OF ROME

THE Roman occupation was one of the most interesting periods in our history, in which the greatest changes were to be effected in our everyday life. For some 367 years, Britain, which was not yet England, was to form part of an Empire which stretched from Babylon, around both sides of the Mediterranean, and up through France to our country. We were to be quite suddenly familiarized with the best which the older European civilization had to offer in the way of Science and Art; and all this wealth of ideas was to be thrust on us when we had not advanced much beyond the stage of being turbulent tribesmen.

Let us look back a little and find out what the Britons were like before the Claudian Conquest of A.D. 43. In *Everyday Life in Prehistoric Times* we finished up with the Glastonbury Lake Village. Here, on a low island in the marshes the inhabitants built wattle and daub huts with thatched roofs, and surrounded these with a stockaded fence. The general appearance must have been that of an East African village today. It had no shape or town-plan; the huts were not set out in any regular arrangement. The whole layout was higgledy-piggledy and haphazard. The people were good craftsmen—could smelt and forge iron, weave, turn wood, and make pottery. The Glastonbury Lake villagers and the inhabitants of other villages all over England, were farmers, able to supply themselves with food and clothing without outside help. But they were not very well organized or very strong and they were always in danger from bands of marauders.

The mere fact of building the Glastonbury Lake Village in a swamp shows that the people must have been afraid, and disaster fell upon them some little time before the Roman occupation. Perhaps they were attacked by the Belgic invaders, who began to arrive in England about 200 B.C., and who seem to have been better organized and equipped with superior weapons of war. But even these Belgic tribes and the other Celtic

19

inhabitants of Britain at the time of the Roman invasion were only small groups of farmers under warlike chieftains. They had in fact fled into England to get out of the way of the Romans who had occupied Gaul (France and part of Germany) a century before, or to avoid other superior tribes of barbarians warring along the frontiers of Civilization. Britain at this time can be compared with the Wild West of America a century ago, when the motto was "go west, young man" and carve out a kingdom for yourself in No Man's Land.

Now think of the feelings of the early Britons as towns like Silchester(6) began to arise in the first century A.D. It must have been an extraordinary experience for them to have watched one of the Roman surveyors at work, and noticed how carefully he set out the town—that it was in fact town-planned; or to see its Basilica(24), with its Corinthian order of architecture, rising from the ground. Or to go to Bath and see the great bathing establishment there, with its lead-lined baths, and intricate plumbing and heating work. The Britons must have heard of the doings of the Romans in Gaul, but probably, like the Queen of Sheba, had not believed, and then when they were confronted with their work, there must have been "no more spirit" in them.

Or take the roads. The two-wheeled chariots of the Britons probably kept to the high ground, and used the trackways which had come down to them from Neolithic times. The lowlands would have been too swampy. Now think of the Roman roads which we still use. We construct laboriously a few miles of arterial roads, or make a by-pass—the Romans covered their Empire with roads which all led to Rome.

Little can be known of the literature of the Britons; doubtless some Homer sang their tribal lays and tales, but no one wrote them down. Nevertheless, their Celtic myths and legends were handed down, and becoming traditional did, in the Middle Ages, develop into a literature peculiarly our own. Against this it must be remembered that the men who arrived here in A.D. 43 were familiar with the masterpieces of Greek and Roman literature. Cicero died in 43 B.C.; Virgil was born in 70 B.C.; and Horace published his Odes in 23 B.C. So the Latin tongue, which was to become a universal language, had already taken form to itself, and was to be heard in our country wherever the Romans came together.

Sir Mortimer Wheeler excavated parts of the Roman city of Verulamium (St. Albans) before the war and this work is being continued year by year as a training school for London University students. Many exciting discoveries have been made in recent years. Here we are concerned with the excavation of the Roman theatre of Verulamium—the only one of its kind in Britain. We hope all our readers will visit this theatre, and it may be as well, before so doing, to study the lie of the land on a map. The Roman Watling Street ran straight through the Roman Verulamium, on its way from St. Stephens, to the south of St. Albans, on to Redbourn, and part of it is now the entrance drive to Gorhambury. So it will be well to steer for St. Michael's Church, about half a mile to the west of St. Albans. Here we shall be in the middle of the old Roman city, in fact, the vicarage of the church is built on the site of its forum, and close by is the theatre.

Fig. 2 shows a reconstruction of the theatre when first built about A.D. 140; it must be taken with a grain of salt. The plan at the side shows the central orchestra, about 80 feet in diameter, and surrounded by a wall. The outer wall, with buttresses, formed the retaining walls for the earth banks, made by sinking the orchestra below the general level. The people sat on wooden seats on the earth banks, and these were reached from external stairs. There were passages down to the orchestra from the outside, and over two of these may have been seats for the notables. The stage occupied only about 48 feet of the perimeter of the orchestra, and behind it was the dressing-room for the actors.

The first thing to be remembered is that this is the only Roman theatre in Britain; and second, that it is more Greek than Roman in plan. Miss Kenyon, however, who has written a very good handbook which can be bought on the site, points out that similar theatres were built in Gaul. All theatres date back to the circular threshing floors, on which the ancient Greeks danced in honour of Dionysus, the god of the vine and fertility, when he had given them a good harvest—that is why the central space is called the orchestra, because it comes from the Greek word to dance.

21

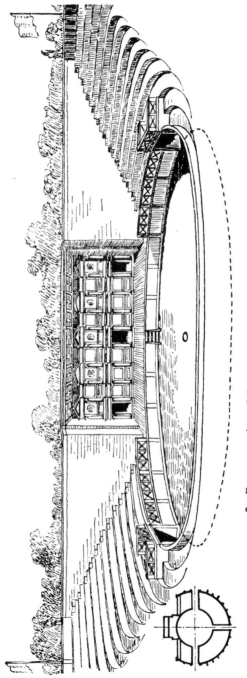

2 Reconstruction of the Roman theatre at Verulamium (St. Albans)

In the sixth and fifth centuries B.C. the Greeks began to produce plays, and so a stage was introduced for the actors. The Romans ordinarily cut the orchestra in half so that it was a semi-circle and much more like a modern theatre. Why did they revert to the Greek type in Britain? Again why did they put a wall round the orchestra at Verulamium? We think that it was because the theatre there was not only used for dances and spectacles, but possible bear-baiting. The orchestra, in fact, was on its way to be turned into the pit. However that may be, go and see the excavations. Another good little book by Mr. Lowther can be bought there, showing the later alterations. Then sadly enough in the fourth century A.D. Britain became so unsettled that there was no time for plays, or even bear-baiting, and the theatre became the midden for the rubbish of a dwindled town.

When we come to the beliefs of the Britons we have more to go on. Caesar wrote, in the Gallic Wars, of the Druidism which was the religion of the later Celtic tribes of Britain and Gaul:

> The whole Gaulish nation is to a great degree devoted to superstitious rites; and on this account those who are afflicted with severe diseases, or who are engaged in battles and dangers, either sacrifice human beings for victims, or vow that they will immolate themselves. These employ the Druids as ministers for such sacrifices, because they think that, unless the life of man be repaid for the life of man, the will of the immortal gods cannot be appeased. Others make wicker-work images of vast size, the limbs of which they fill with living images and set on fire.

It is a common error to associate the Druids with Stonehenge, but this had been built nearly 2000 years before. The Romans were tolerant of the beliefs of those whom they conquered, but Druidism seems to have shocked even the Romans, until they finally destroyed it in its headquarters at Anglesey.

What makes our period for ever memorable is that the Roman occupation began soon after the birth of Our Lord. Christ was born in Palestine, and here it was, and in Asia Minor, that the greater part of the work of the Apostles was carried out. It is the tradition at Glastonbury that Joseph of Arimathea came there about A.D. 47, bringing with him a cup in which he had caught the last drops of Christ's blood, and this having been lost, the search for the Holy Grail became the great work of Arthur and his knights.

There must have been Christian legionaries, and in any case, after the Edict of Toleration in 313, they were free to worship in their own way. Figs. *13–15* illustrate the probable Christian Church at Silchester. From the blazing wicker images of the Druids to the Sermon on the Mount, preached at Silchester, is a revolutionary happening of prime importance to a Christian people.

In this period, then, our people were subjected to the three great civilizing influences in European civilization—the teaching of Greece, Rome, and Christianity.

There is an amusing idea that the Romans arrived here in A.D. 43, and departed in A.D. 410, during which time, 367 years, they kept themselves to themselves. That is equal to a period from the early days of Elizabeth's reign to 1937. Unless the legionary was quite unlike all other soldiers, it is probable that many of them fell in love with and married British maidens; so some of us, if we did but know, may have had Roman forbears. We know one Scotsman whose profile we have seen on Roman coins, and of course the Roman legionaries were recruited from all corners of the Empire—from the plains of Hungary and North Germany, from the Tigris and from North Africa. One Roman emperor was a Negro. So that a considerable amount of new blood entered the British racial stock during the Roman occupation, as at all other times in their long history.

We hope we have given enough examples to show that the Roman occupation of Gaul and Britain was not a trivial happening, but the broad base on which, after the Dark Ages, Western Europe was able to rebuild her foundations. The development of Gothic and Renaissance styles was derived from the memories of Rome, but this does not explain why, when the Romans came here in A.D. 43, they had so much to offer us. It is here that the romance of the period comes in. The great central fact about the Roman civilization is that by their earlier conquests they had inherited the wisdom of the ancient Near East, Egypt and Babylonia, the Israelites and Assyrians, the Minoans, Mycenaeans, and Achaeans; the Medes and Persians had all in their time contributed to a civilization which made its supreme bid for power, and met its defeat at the hands of the Greeks at Salamis in 480 B.C. When the Romans conquered the Greeks, a great fund of knowledge, which was becoming scientific and systematic, was placed at their disposal.

We begin with the popular modern subject of town-planning. Hippodamus of Miletus laid out Piraeus, the port of Athens, in the fifth century B.C. in a rectangular plane, and Alexander the Great was a town-planner. Dinocrates, his architect, laid out Alexandria (page 28).

The Romans were not only very good planners, as we can see by fig. 6 of Silchester, but they paid great attention to public health and sanitation. They constructed sewers; the Cloaca Maxima in Rome can still be traced from the Forum of Nerva to its outflow into the Tiber. So far as medicine is concerned, Hippocrates, the great Greek doctor, was born as early as 460 B.C., and seems to have practised this profession as a doctor does today, with an outlook which was scientific and free from quackery. The earliest scientific medical work of the Romans seems to have been *De re Medica* of Celsus, about 30 B.C. This deals with the history of medicine, diet, disease, dentistry, and difficult and dangerous operations. The Roman bath at Bath was not only a bathing establishment but the earliest known English medical cure.

If we turn to architecture the Roman debt to the Greeks is equally apparent. The Greeks evolved their three Orders of Architecture(*3–5*); if we turn to figs. *18–21*, we shall find that the Romans adopted their "orders", altering them somewhat in detail, and adding one more(*20*), the Composite, which was a fusion of Ionic and Corinthian, and these orders are still used.

Our Christian churches can be traced back to the Roman basilica, as described on page 38. There is hardly anything which we do today which cannot be traced back to Greece through Rome.

A very interesting day could be spent in a visit to the Glastonbury Museum, where are all the primitive things which were discovered in the Lake Village. An hour's run in the car would take us to the great Roman bathing establishment of the Romans at Bath(*12*)—an amazing contrast to Glastonbury. In the afternoon, there would be time to go to Bradford-on-Avon

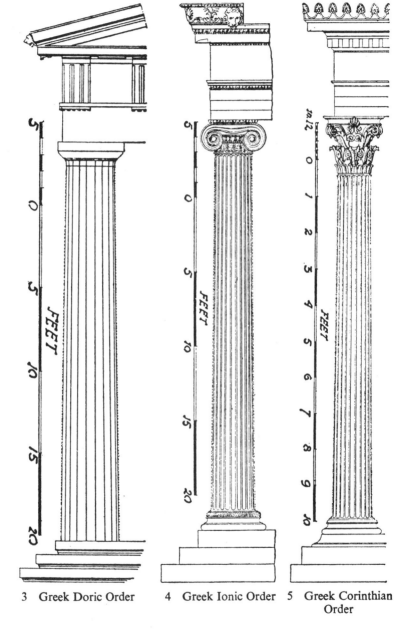

3 Greek Doric Order   4 Greek Ionic Order   5 Greek Corinthian
Order

and see the little Saxon church there. Centuries had to pass before the Saxons were able to build even such a simple structure as this. There could be no better illustration of the meaning of the Dark Ages which followed the fall of Rome—from the glory that was Greece to the grandeur that was Rome, and then back to this simple little church. Still, out of it Gothic architecture did develop. And then, while in Bradford, we could see The Hall there—an Elizabethan home which shows a renaissance of classical detail even more. A bird's-eye view, or pageant if you will, of the development of English architecture, and all to be seen in one day, in one small corner of England, by those who have the eyes to see.

Chapter II

SILCHESTER AND THE OTHER ROMAN TOWNS

C ALLEVA ATREBATUM, Calleva (the town in the wood) of the Atrebates(6) was planned on regular symmetrical lines. Silchester, as we call it now, was town-planned, and here for the first time we meet the chequer-board type of planning in this country. It presents a marked difference to the plan of Glastonbury Lake Village, which we saw in *Prehistoric Times*, fig. *139*; there it was haphazard arrangement, with less sense of order.

If we try to trace the evolution of the chess-board type of plan, we are led back from Rome to Greece, and the work of Alexander the Great. He was a great town-planner, and his influence can be traced in the design of the cities of Asia Minor. The straight streets commended themselves to the soldier, because this was the manner in which he was accustomed to lay out his camps. In Roman times the soldier was much more than a mere fighter; he was, in fact, the handyman of the day, and could plan a town, build walls, and carry out engineering works. When Roman soldiers retired it was a practice to gather them together, and grant them land, as a reward for their services; then they built a town, and became a bulwark to the State; Timgad in the province of Numidia, in Roman Africa, was such a city. In more ways than one the power of Rome depended on its legionaries, and we like to think of them, when their fighting days were over, building and carpentering, and showing the natives that their strong arms were attached to cunning hands.

It is quite evident that the Romans, wherever they went for their inspirations, were accomplished surveyors. No matter how well a road is made and finished, it has to be begun by someone, who determines its direction, and settles the gradients; a town cannot be laid out until men come along and peg out the lines

28

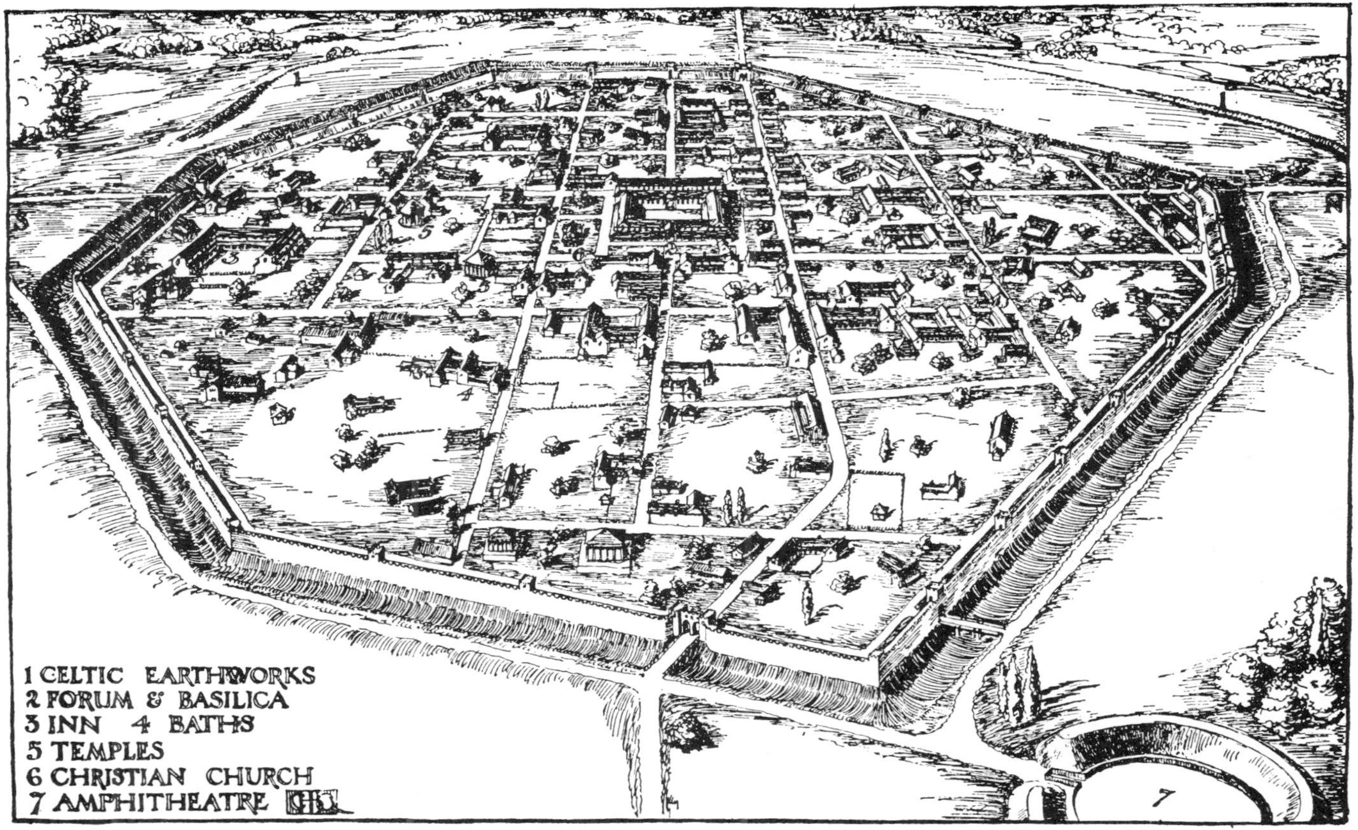

1 CELTIC EARTHWORKS
2 FORUM & BASILICA
3 INN 4 BATHS
5 TEMPLES
6 CHRISTIAN CHURCH
7 AMPHITHEATRE

6 Silchester (Calleva Atrebatum)

of its streets and walls. This brings up the question of mensuration. The surveyor must instruct the constructor; he must say, for example, "Here is the main street of your town, it is so many somethings wide."

In these days of plenty, we are accustomed to travel about with bulging pockets, full of rules, rods, and tape measures, but this was not the case in the days long before Rome. Men used something which they could always be sure of having with them, to wit, their feet, and by Roman times, this habit had passed from custom into law. Vitruvius, writing in the time of Augustus said: "It is worthy of remark, that the measures necessarily used in all buildings and other works, are derived from the members of the human body, as the digit, the palm, the foot, the cubit." The normal Roman foot was 296 mm., or a full 11⅝ English inches. There were 16 digits, and 4 palms in the Roman foot, and the cubit was 6 palms, or 1½ feet. Five Roman feet went to the *passus* (pace), and 1000 of the latter to the mile.

In the same way the numerals have been derived from the hand with its five fingers. The Roman V is thought to have been simplified from a drawing of the hand meaning 5. IV would mean the hand less one finger, or 4; and VI the hand plus one or 6, and X a double hand or 10.

When it came to measuring land, the Roman thought of the feet of his oxen rather than his own, so the unit he used was the iugerum, or yokeland; the oxen ploughed a furrow 120 Roman feet long, before they wanted a rest, and 120 by 120 formed the actus. Two square actus, or 120 by 240, was the day's ploughing, and this became the iugerum, which was the unit of the Roman land surveyor. The Roman dealt in land in blocks, which he could size up in his mind, and readily estimate the crops which could be grown. Mensuration, as most other subjects, is full of interest, if you go to work to discover it. Here in England, our furlong is a furrow long, equal to one eighth of a mile, or 40 rods, poles, or perches; this rod unit of 16½ feet has played a great part in English mensuration, and we shall have something to say of it later on.

ROMAN MEASUREMENTS

Below we have set out in tabular form the Roman measures:

Feet.	Gradus.	Passus.	Decempeda.	Actus.	Iugerum.	Stadium.	Mile.
2½ =	1						
5 =	2 =	1					
10 =	4 =	2 =	1				
120 =	48 =	24 =	12	=1			
240 =	96 =	48 =	24	=2	=1		
625 =	250 =	125				=1	
5000 =	2000 =	1000 =	500				=1

and the Roman mile was just over 1618 English yards.

In founding a Roman city, the plough was used to trace the outline of its walls, and it was inaugurated by the augur, who consecrated the templum, or centre square; here the cardo, running from north to south, was crossed by the decumanus from east to west. The four quarters of the town, around these main streets, were divided up into rectangular blocks, of which the iugerum was the general unit.

The surveyor, who was responsible for the layout of the city, used an instrument called the groma (7). This consisted of a staff, with a cross turning on its top, from the ends of which small plummets were suspended by cords. These plummets came at the corners of a square, and it was the cords by which they were suspended that were used to sight the lines the surveyor wished to set out. His method was to send his assistants to hold rods which were stuck in the ground, where they were sighted as being on the line. It is obvious that the square line that the Romans liked so much could be set out very readily. Once the lines

7   Roman surveyors (Agrimensores or Gromatici) using the groma

31

were set out, a 10-foot rod was used, and 12 of these gave the actus of 120 feet, Surveyors today use an instrument founded on the groma, which they call a cross-head staff.

Silchester (6) was not a Roman municipality. There seem to have been only six of these in Britain, four of which were colonial (colonies of veteran soldiers)—Camulodunum (Colchester), Lindum (Lincoln), Glevum (Gloucester), Eburacum (York)—and two municipia (specially recognised settlements already in existence)—Verulamium (St. Albans) and, probably, Rotis (Leicester). The remainder of the country, except for imperial estates such as the lead mines of the Mendips, was organised in civitates which followed approximately the old tribal divisions, with the chiefs as magistrates. Local self-government was encouraged everywhere, and the main difference between these civitates and the municipalities was that the members of the latter were Roman citizens. The distinction, however, ceased to have real meaning when in 212 the Emperor Caracalla gave Roman citizenship to all freeborn provincials. Silchester must have been the civitas of the Atrebates. The town was rebuilt in its Roman form, with chessboard regularity, at about the end of the first and beginning of the second centuries, and, situated as it is (1), on the top of a rounded hill, in pleasant country, and at the intersection of busy roads, must have been a place of importance.

Let us imagine that we are paying a visit to Calleva Atrebatum. We approach the town by the road from the north, and on the outskirts we pass a funeral party going to bury its dead, outside the walls at the side of the road as was the Roman custom. Close up to the town, at 1, fig. 6, is a ditch and bank, which may be the remains of the old British earthworks that had surrounded the tribal stronghold long before the days of the Romans. Like many British earthworks, these banks and ditches follow the contour lines of the hill, and are not square. The British earthworks influenced the layout of the stone walls, which were added at some later date than the rebuilding in Roman times; thus the streets are Roman in their chequer pattern, and the walls are British in their plan.

As we pass along outside the walls, we notice that they are about 20 feet high, built of concrete rubble, and faced with flints; they are strengthened with bonding courses of ironstone,

8   The West Gate of Silchester

and finished at the bottom with chamfered stone bases. There
are rampart walks on the tops of the walls, with embrasures
through which the watchmen can see the approach of strangers;
at the base of the wall is a ditch 12 feet deep and 80 feet
wide.

When we are inside the walls, we shall find that these are
9 feet 6 inches broad at base, lessened by set-offs inside to
about 7 feet 6 inches at the top, and at about 200 feet intervals
the full thickness of the wall is carried up, like a wide buttress,
and on these are placed watch towers. To further strengthen
the walls, a mound of earth has been placed against them
inside.

By this time we have arrived at the West Gate (8). The town,
or curtain, walls are curved inwards on to two towers, and so
take the form of bastions, from which the bridge over the ditch
can be raked. Between the towers are double archways of 12
feet span, at 1 on the plan; at 2 is a guard-room, with a lock-up

33

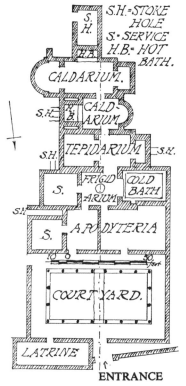

S.H.=STOKE HOLE
S.=SERVICE
H.B.=HOT BATH.

CALDARIUM.

S.H. CALD- ARIUM

S.H. TEPIDARIUM S.H.

FRIGID ARIUM COLD BATH

S.

S. APODYTERIA

COURTYARD.

LATRINE

ENTRANCE

9   Plan of the Baths at Silchester

behind it at 3. The other side of the plan is at the rampart level, and shows how the guard can pass from the top of the walls at 4, through the towers at 5, and over the archways at 6.

If we now pass through the gate, it may be as well to consult fig. 6, and imagine that it is the plan of Calleva Atrebatum, scratched in a tablet which has been lent to us by the keeper of the gate. We will follow the road which goes due east, until it crosses another running from the North to the South Gate, and here we will turn to the right. Almost immediately, at 2 on the plan, we shall come to a building, which by its size shows itself to be a place of importance, and on inquiry we find that it is the basilica; however, we will defer our inspection of the city until we have found an inn at which we can stay, and by consulting our map we see that there is one a little way ahead at 3.

The inn turns out to be a place rather like the house we describe on page 56, except that it has more accommodation, and has baths attached. We hear that there are larger baths, at 4 on the plan; so after leaving our bags at the inn, we go on to these, so that we may refresh ourselves after our journey.

Fig. 9 shows the plan of the building we find there. We enter a courtyard with a colonnaded walk around it, and this leads into the apodyteria, or dressing-rooms; here we take off our clothes and give our valuables into the care of an attendant. We then go into the frigidarium, or cold room; here we see men who

10
Strigil

34

have finished their baths, plunging into the cold bath, so that they may not catch cold on going into the open air; our readers know, of course, that the Roman bath consists of going into a series of rooms, heated with hot air, and this heat induces very generous perspiration.

We next enter the tepidarium which is fairly warm, and then the caldarium, which is really quite hot; here there is a bath of hot water, and at one end a basin of cold water, with which to splash oneself before passing out. It is here that we are anointed with oils, and our bodies massaged and scraped with strigils; then we, in our turn, pass back to the frigidarium and have our cold plunge, and sit about to watch the goings-on. Seneca, the philosopher, writing about A.D. 57, gives a better idea of life as seen in a Roman bath than we can. He said:

I am living near a bath: sounds are heard on all sides. Just imagine for yourself every conceivable kind of noise that can offend the ear. The men of more sturdy muscle go through their exercises, and swing their hands heavily weighted with lead: I hear their groans when they strain themselves, or the whistling of laboured breath when they breathe out after having held in. If one is rather lazy, and merely has himself rubbed with unguents, I hear the blows of the hand slapping his shoulders, the sound varying according as the massagist strikes with flat or hollow palm. If a ball-player begins to play and to count his throws it's all up for the time being, (then follows an amusing note) or there is some one in the bath who loves to hear the sound of his own voice. . . . but the hair-plucker from time to time raises his thin shrill voice in order to attract attention, and is only still himself when he is forcing cries of pain from some one else, from whose armpits he plucks the hairs.

Fig. *11* shows the exterior of the baths at Silchester, and for a small town they are fine buildings, unless, of course, they are compared with those at Bath, or Aquae Sulis. Here the hot springs of healing waters have been conducted to great basins in which the people can bathe, and grouped around these are the ordinary rooms of a Roman bath as at Silchester. We give a sketch(*12*) of the Great Bath, taken from the east end. So far as we can judge this bathing-pool must have been open to the sky when it was first built, with a colonnaded walk around, as at A on the sketch. Later it was roofed in with a vault made of

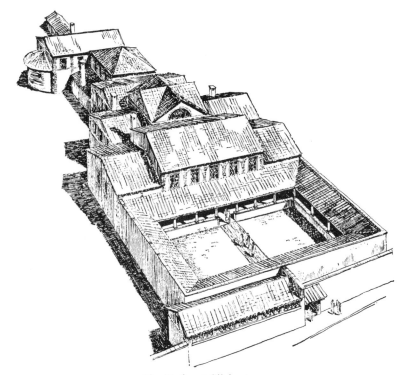

11   Baths at Silchester

concrete reinforced with hollow tiles, and to carry this, large stone piers were added at B. By cross vaults the architect contrived that these piers at B took all the weight of the vault, adding arches at the back to take up any outward thrust; these were carried on piers, one of which is shown at C.

The parts remaining of this vault at Bath give the best example we have in England of the Roman use of concrete reinforced with brickwork. In Rome itself the baths of Diocletian and Caracalla, the basilica of Constantine, and the Pantheon, are examples of vaults which are wonderful in their immense scale and permanence. It is very doubtful if any of the modern concrete work, reinforced with steel, will last even one hundred years against the insidious rust.

After our bath, being in good order, we go to the church, there

12   The Great Bath at Bath

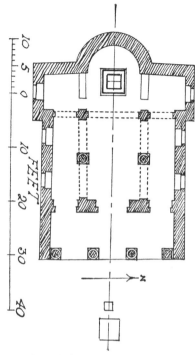

13 Plan of the Christian church at Silchester

to return thanks for our safe journey, and we find that the citizens of Calleva, very soon after the Edict of Toleration of the Emperor Constantine in 313, set about building themselves a Christian church. This is shown at 6 on fig. 6.

The plan of the church (13) is of what is known as the "basilican type", which means that it resembles the basilica(24). The points of resemblance are that the main body is divided into a nave, with an aisle on each side, and the tribune of the basilica has become the apse of the church. The plan shows the beginning of transepts, which give the church its cruciform, or cross-like character.

It is worth considering how this came about. Take a sheet of paper and try to design anything you like; you may start with the idea that you are going to be wildly original, and then you will discover that originality consists of minute variations and improvements on what has gone before, and you will be forced to go back to something you know as a base on which to build. This is precisely what the first builders of Christian churches did; they started by adopting the basilica, because it was the building in which they had been used to assemble; the interest to us is that the little church at Silchester is the forerunner of our glorious Gothic cathedrals.

We must remember that the Society of Antiquaries, who excavated Silchester, only discovered the foundations of the building; the reconstruction built on these is our own. We will enter the church, and our first impression(15) is one of surprise at the tiny size of the building; the nave, including the apse, is only 29 feet long by 10 feet wide; the aisles are 5 feet wide. The nave has a mosaic floor, the tesserae of which are red tiles 1 inch square; where the altar stands is a very beautiful panel of chequers in black, red, and white, and this part of the floor is not raised above the nave.

Let us now leave our imaginary walk and look at the drawings. Fig. *14* is a reconstruction, built up on the plan about which there is no doubt. For the superstructure, we have gone to Rome. After Constantine's Edict of Toleration, church building went forward, and the Christians had no need to lurk in byways. It is to this period that we can assign the five patriarchal basilicas, of St. Peter, St. John Lateran, Ste. Maria Maggiore, St. Paul, and St. Lorenzo, beyond the walls at Rome. The old basilica of St. Peter was pulled down at the end of the fifteenth century to make room for the present church, and the others have been altered many times, yet sufficient remains to show what the early churches were like. Constantine is supposed to have helped dig the foundations of St. John Lateran with his own hands.

The Silchester church was a much simpler building; its flint walls, with tile angles outside, were plastered inside, and painted in imitation of marble.

During Mass the priest stood facing eastwards behind the altar, which was probably a wooden table.

In the larger basilican churches it was usual for the clergy to be seated around the apse behind the altar, but there is hardly room for this arrangement at Silchester, and they probably

14   Exterior of the church at Silchester

15   Interior of the church at Silchester

used the nave together with the choir. Men and women were seated separately in the aisles. It will be noticed that there is a very large porch, or narthex. Here, with the doors open, were gathered the people not yet admitted to full communion.

This narthex, in the larger basilican churches, like St. Peter's, formed one side of a square courtyard, or atrium, which stood in front of the church. There is a splendid example at the later church of St. Ambrogio in Milan, and another delightful one at St. Clemente in Rome.

We cannot be sure if there was such a court at Silchester, but a foundation was discovered in front of the porch, with a little pit behind it, and this is thought to have been the base on which stood a laver, or labrum, where the worshippers could wash their hands, the pit having a drain connected with it. This laver may have been placed centrally in an eastern court, paved with flint pitching, of which part remains. Silchester church was built between 313 and the withdrawal of the Romans about a century later, and a similar building has been found at Caerwent (Venta Silurum) in Monmouthshire.

Here and there in England, smaller Christian relics of Roman date have been discovered. One of the most interesting of these is the pewter bowl in the British Museum, discovered in the well of a Roman house at Appleshaw, near Andover, not far from Silchester. This bowl has the sacred monogram, Chi-Rho, composed of the two first Greek letters of the name Christ(*16*) engraved on its base.

Apart from the town churches or basilicas, built specifically for Christian worship, we know something of how the needs of Christians were served in rural districts from the excavations at the Roman villa at Lullingstone in Kent. Here two or more rooms appear to have been set aside for Christian use during the fourth century. Fragments of painted wall plaster also decorated with the sacred Chi-Rho monogram have been found, and also figures of saints or pilgrims with their arms extended on either side in the early Christian attitude of prayer.

There are hints, in writings of the period, of British converts to Christianity early in

16 Sacred Monogram, Chi-Rho

73'·0"

17 One of the temples at Silchester

the third century. St. Alban was martyred in 304, and three British bishops attended the Council of Arles in 314, which is evidence that, by this time, the converts had organized a Church. Then we have St. Patrick, the 1462nd anniversary of whose death was recognized on March 17th, 1924 by the dedication of a mosaic to his memory in the Houses of Parliament at Westminster. St. Patrick's name was Sucat, and he was the son of Calpurnius, a Roman official, who was a deacon of the Church, and whose father had been a priest.

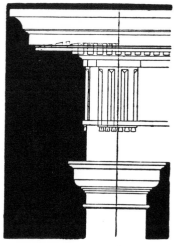

18   Roman Doric Order
(theatre of Marcellus, Rome)

St. Patrick was born about 373, either in Dumbarton, or Glamorganshire, and was carried off by slave raiders to Ireland when a youth. Here he stayed six years, and then escaped to Gaul, whence, being trained in the Church, he went to Rome,

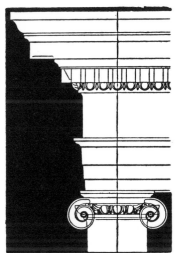

19   Roman Ionic Order
(theatre of Marcellus, Rome)

and finally returned on his mission to the Irish about 437 or 438, where the Christians stood in need of his help.

We shall write later of the influence of the Irish Church, but sufficient has been said now to show that the Christian Church in this country was not the work of Augustine only.

There were four temples at Silchester in pre-Christian days, and these are shown at 5, fig. 6. Fig. 17 illustrates one of these near the East Gate. During the excavations of the Society of Antiquaries, the foundations of a platform, 73 feet square,

43

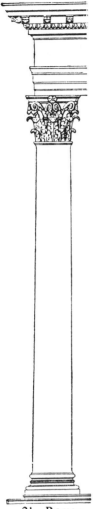

21 Roman
Corinthian Order
(Portico of Pan-
theon, Rome)

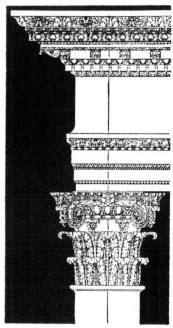

20   Roman Composite Order
(Arch of Titus, Rome)

were discovered. The platform itself was 7½ feet high, and in the middle of it stood the cella, which was 42 feet square outside, and 36 feet inside. The drawing is our reconstruction based on this plan.

The foundations of what must have been a very beautiful and interesting temple were discovered to the south of the basilica. The platform here had a regular 16-sided plan of 65 feet diameter. The cella placed centrally on this was 35 feet 7 inches in diameter, with walls which were 2 feet 6 inches thick, and 16-sided externally. This left space for the cella to be surrounded by a colonnaded walk or peristyle, 9 feet 6 inches wide, and the effect must have been like the temple of Vesta at Tivoli, or the beautiful one in the Forum Boarium at Rome.

44

THE ROMAN ORDERS

Now that we are writing of temples, it may be well to make reference to the Orders of Architecture which the Romans used in their construction. We illustrated those of the Greeks on page 26. The Romans adopted them, but changed them as they went along. The Doric(*18*) from the theatre of Marcellus at Rome, has been used in figs. *14* and *17*. The Ionic, also from the theatre of Marcellus, was as fig. *19*. The Corinthian, from the Pantheon, Rome, was as fig. *21*; and the Composite, from the Arch of Titus, Rome(*20*) was, as its name shows, composed of a fusion of Ionic and Corinthian. These Orders, together with the arch, were the raw materials with which the Roman architect worked, and his finished products, in the way of buildings, are the main inspiration of his successor of today.

If it had been possible for us to walk the streets of Roman Silchester, as we at first pretended, after breakfasting at our inn we should go to the basilica to transact the business which brought us to the town. The basilica, as we have seen(*6*, 2), stood in the centre of the east side of the street running through the town from north to south; if we go two islands to the west, and two to the east, and then take two north and south, we find that the streets are planned on a regular square. If Silchester had been a purely Roman town, this square would have been walled in, as was Caerwent in Monmouthshire, close to Caerleon, where the Second Legion was stationed. It rather looks as if this central portion at Silchester was the first portion built, as early as A.D. 70–85, and the walls, enclosing about 100 acres, were built at a later date to follow the lines of the British earthworks.

The broadest roads in the town were about 28½ feet wide, and formed of a bed of hard gravel, pitched with flints in the centre, to form a gutter.

The basilica formed part of a group of buildings(*22*). This plan is very remarkable and shows us that the Romans were quite used to buildings planned on an axial line, with a sense of dignity and order. We know that there had not been any such building done in England before the time of the Romans, and after them we have to wait till the sixteenth century before we find these ideas again.

The gateway(*22*, 1), led into the forum, or Greek agora(*23*). This was the market place of the town, and around it were

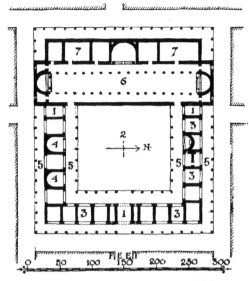

22   Plan of the forum and basilica at Silchester

shops(22, 3). Here the slaves came to do their marketing, and the country people set up little booths. It was used as well for games, and gladiatorial contests before the amphitheatre was built. The municipal offices were at 4, and colonnaded walks at 5. These connected with the basilica at 6. This consisted of a fine hall, about 233 feet long by 58 feet wide; here the merchants met to do business, as they do at the "Baltic" today. At each end were the semicircular tribunes where justice was administered. In the centre of the west side was the curia, or the council chamber of the city, with other halls and offices, at 7.

Fig. 24 shows what the interior of the basilica looked like. This reconstruction is possible because part of one of the Corinthian capitals was found, and this settled the diameter of the columns. In Roman architecture the height of a column bears a definite relation to its diameter, and again the entablature over, consisting of architrave, frieze, and cornice, has a definite proportion. During the excavations, portions of Purbeck marble and an imported white marble were found, and it is thought that these were used for wall linings. The portions not treated in this way were plastered, and painted gaily with light red, yellow, white, blue, and green. The world has only become grey in colour since the Industrial Revolution.

We will here insert a reminder that before the Christian era, a basilica was a place such as we have described, but that after, the word was used at times for a church.

This group of buildings, in more ways than one, formed the

46

civic centre. It is interesting to remember that the word civilization comes from *civis*, a citizen, one who had mastered the art of living in a town. The Atrebates seem to have managed it very well; better, in fact, than we do today, with our hopeless struggle to make the dreadful industrial towns fit places in which to live.

During the excavations no trace of buildings was found to the south of the basilica, behind the church. This space may have been the cattle market, and another open space on the east may have been used for the farmers' carts.

Silchester does not provide us with a specimen of one of the great accomplishments of the Romans, the arched bridge. It is a great pity that they did not feel tempted to span the Thames with bridges like the Pons Ælius and Pons Fabricius at Rome.

Before we study the smaller details of Silchester, it would be as well if we again looked at its layout (6), and consider what it means. True, there are the later walls, added when times were becoming troublous, but even with these it presents a very civilized picture. It is not dominated by a castle, with moat and drawbridges, as was the case with the towns which were built in the Middle Ages. The people of Silchester may have needed protection from raiders, but nobody frowned at them from inside. Here they were able to lead a life which was free, and gave them opportunities to develop their own individual tastes. Later the Barbarian raids forced men together in packs, and a common fear made them wolfish; the monastery was to become the one place in which a man could do quiet work, and the cloak of religion the only substitute for a sharp sword. The world had to wait a thousand years or more before it was to see again any town planned on such kindly lines as Silchester.

23   The forum and basilica at Silchester

24 The interior of the basilica, Silchester

VIROCONIUM

Viroconium, like Silchester, was a great Roman town in which the British element is evident in the nature of its plan, and in other ways; but both its beginning and its end are wrapped in mystery. It is thought to have been the base from which the attack on the Ordovices of North Wales was launched, a base which was later moved to Chester (Deva), where the great fortress was built, which was occupied for so long by the Twentieth Legion. As to its end, the general opinion is that it was sudden, overwhelming, and tragic, an onslaught by fire and sword. One of the most startling clues to this idea was found in the heating chamber of the baths, where, among the small forest of pillars which carried the floor of the heated room above the floor of the furnace chamber some skeletons were found huddled together. They had evidently been suffocated by the fumes. That they had come here as a last resort to escape from a worse death, was seen by the fact that they had brought their small store of earthly treasure with them—the skeleton of an old man still clutched a bag of coins. The disaster is placed in the fifth century, but whether the enemy was the Pict, the Scot, or the Saxon is unknown.

As at Silchester, no town was ever again built on the site of Viroconium. The village of Wroxeter stands to one side of the ruined city, and is but a tiny place. But much of the church is built with material from the Roman buildings, and the font is hollowed out of an upturned base from one of the columns of the forum. Silchester, as we have seen (page 28), was a town of the British tribe Atrebates; Viroconium was a town of the Cornovii, as is clearly set forth in the finest lettered inscription ever found in Britain, whose place was over the entrance to the forum. Out of the great quantity of things found here, one of the most interesting is a soldier's discharge-book. It is not quite a book in our sense of the word, being graven on a small sheet of copper. But it evidently answered the same purpose as the discharge-book which is handed to the present-day soldier when his time of service in the army is expired. It runs as follows:

The Emperor, Caesar Trajanus Hadrianus Augustus, son of the deified Trajanus, grandson of the deified Nerva, Chief Pontiff, holding the Tribuncian Power for the nineteenth time. Consul for the third time, Father of his Country.
To THE Cavalry and Infantry who have served in six cavalry

49

regiments and thirty-one infantry regiments which are called—
(names given but many indecipherable) and are in Britain under
Publius Mummius Sisenna; who have served for twenty-five or
more years, and have been discharged with an honourable
discharge, whose names are written below:—HAS GIVEN citizenship
for themselves, their children, and their descendants, and the right
of legal marriage with the wives they then possessed when citizenship was given to them, or if any of them are bachelors with those
whom they may hereafter marry up to the number of one apiece.

April 14th

In the Consulship of L. Tutilius Pontianus and C. Calpurnius
Atilianus (A.D. 135).

Of the Second Cohort of Dalmatians commanded by . . . Julius
Maximus of Rome.

To the ex-footsoldier

Mansuetus, son of Lucius of the neighbourhood of Trier.

Copied and checked from the bronze tablet which is fixed in
Rome on the wall behind the temple of the deified Augustus near
Minerva's temple.

So runs this magnificent rigmarole which is a certified true
copy of a bronze tablet put up in Rome—such was the efficiency
of the Records Department of the War Office of ancient Rome.
Every soldier honourably discharged had such a tablet erected
and could have a certified true copy to keep by him if he chose
to pay for it. When the present document in copper was prepared,
one can sense from the couching of the official language how
the ex-foot-soldier, Mansuetus, son of Lucius, was much the
least important person mentioned. Yet, after all these years, it
is his name alone which fires our imagination, because he has
presented himself to us as a personality (if a very ordinary one)
with a name, who lived in that long-forgotten city of Britain.
Here is a man *with a name* who lived in old Wroxeter eighteen
hundred years ago! We know a little more from the date and the
various regiments quoted (and some of these proud fighting
units we should never have heard of but for Mansuetus). We
know, for instance, that he served as a member of the garrison
in that fort on Hadrian's Wall which in his time was called
Magnae and is now called Carvoran. Magnae is ruined, Viroconium buried, the Empire vanished. But this scrap certifying

the honourable discharge of Mansuetus, son of Lucius, is still with us, as good as new, and it may outlast the skyscrapers of New York, concrete though they be.

In Viroconium one may perhaps trace something of the answer to that interesting riddle of *how a town comes to be*. If our guess is right that the attack on North Wales was launched from here, and that the Romans had at first intended the fort they founded here to be the home of a legion (though the plan was changed and Chester made the legionary fortress), then we have the nucleus. After the foundation of Chester, Viroconium would have a double reason for prosperity. For the natural resources of the countryside of Shropshire are rich, and the garrison at Chester, although some forty miles away, would afford it a measure of protection. Now, although the town was wiped out (as we guess) and its site became a desert, the tradition and the developed system of its trade was evidently not lost. These were merely transferred to an adjacent site better protected by natural barriers. The new location chosen was at the bend of the Severn, where the river forms an isthmus, then known as Pengwern and now called Shrewsbury; and its motto, *Floreat Salopia*, still holds good.

Another interesting example of a civil town with something akin in its history is to be seen in South Wales. This is Venta Silurum, now called Caerwent. It also has a neighbour in a great legionary fortress, namely, that at Caerleon (Isca Silurum), but the distance in this case is only a matter of seven miles. Though the buildings at Caerwent have mostly been excavated there is less to see there than at Viroconium, except for one grand feature which is lost to view in the Shropshire town. That is the walls. The south and west walls at Caerwent are one of the best examples of their kind in Britain. In some respects they are unique, and they are now preserved as an ancient monument by the Ministry of Works. What the fate of this town was after the end of the Roman occupation of Britain is not known. Probably it was not so sudden and disastrous as that of Viroconium. But in spite of its walls it came to an end as a trade centre, though there seems to be good evidence that here again there was a transfer and the business faculty moved from Caerwent to Chepstow.

Caerleon (Caerwent's neighbour) was the home of the Second

Legion. And, as was the custom at an important garrison town, there was an amphitheatre in which fights with wild beasts and between gladiators were "put on". Recent excavations have unearthed this building, which has been wonderfully preserved. The entrance, the dens of the beasts, are all to be seen. It is far the best example which we have. It is not the biggest, for that is at Chester, but excavation is here impossible because of the town.

At Colchester the Roman walls of the town are wonderfully well preserved. And here is to be seen the most perfect specimen which we have of a Roman gateway. At Colchester, too, is our only ruin of a large temple. It is very fragmentary, however, consisting only of the vaults of the foundation, for on top of it is built a Norman castle, the whole material of which is of Roman origin. There are many ruins of small temples that were raised to the gods of the British, but of the larger sort dedicated to the gods and the god-emperors of the official religion of Rome no remains exist except this single one at Colchester—it is thought to have been raised to the conqueror of Britain, the deified Emperor Claudius.

Colchester was the old chief metropolis of Britain before the Romans made London. Here reigned Cunobelinus, the Cymbeline of Shakespeare, father of Caractacus. And at Lexden, on the outskirts of Colchester, a tumulus has been excavated which contained the remains of so rich and grand a funeral that it could have been the grave of Cunobelinus himself.

Chapter III

THE PEOPLE AND THEIR HOUSES

THE time has come to write about the people who lived in these towns. We have set out our stage, and the drawings we have made must be accepted as the scenery. Against this background we will place our figures, but, alas, we cannot endow them with life, nor even jerk them with little strings, as marionettes, from the top of the stage. The imaginations of our readers must supply the motive power.

Fig. *102* shows some of the people one might have seen in a walk round Silchester in Roman times. The central couple is a higher magistrate and his wife. He wears the toga prætexta, made of white wool, with a purple border, which was worn as well by priests, and freeborn children until they grew up. Under the toga came the tunica, with the purple border if the wearer was a senator. The toga developed from the cloak, which in early times had been the national garment, and in the Empire was the ceremonial dress of the upper classes. Linen was not used before the Empire.

Fig. *25* shows how the toga was put on. About 6 feet of the straight edge was placed over the left shoulder, the curved side being outside; the remaining part of the toga was passed round the body, under the right arm, and then thrown over the left shoulder as 2. The part which hung down in front from the left shoulder was then pulled up under the fold across the body as 3. Women wore the stola, a form of tunica, with an undershift (*subucula*), and their mantle was an oblong-shaped piece of material which was worn as the left-hand figure in fig. *102*. This was the palla. The tunica was

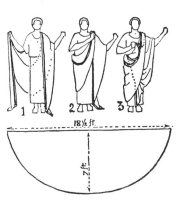

25 Pattern and method of putting-on of the toga

53

26   Hair-dressing

the indoor garment for men and women; sometimes, as shown on the central woman in fig. *102*, it was sleeveless, and then the undershift had sleeves.

Rough tunics were worn by shop-keepers and workmen, like the left-hand man shown in our drawing, and we must bear in mind that mingling with the crowd we should have met in Silchester would have been figures wearing the old British costume we described in *Prehistoric Times*. The right-hand pair of figures are clothed in this way, but the man wears in addition the hooded cloak (*paenula*), a very useful outdoor garment. This hood was to remain until in the fourteenth century it was lengthened into the liripipe, hanging from the chaperon, and finished by snuggling down into a turban.

As well as sandals, heavy leather shoes studded with nails were worn. Fig. *26* shows a method of hair-dressing which was fashionable in the days of the early Empire, and fig. *27* is a carved bone pin which may have been used for the hair.

In *Prehistoric Times* we traced the very beautiful developments of the brooch (*fibula*): how, from a simple safety-pin, it became a very elaborate affair with bi-lateral springs. These continued in Roman times, but in the early Empire we find hinged brooches (*28*). The ones illustrated were made of bronze, and then tinned to look like silver.

Had we been walking round Silchester in Roman times, we should not have found all the people in togas to be pure Romans, and those in tunics, Britons. If we remember how small a State was the original Rome, we can see that there would not have been enough Romans to go round. One of the ways in which the genius of the Romans was shown

27 Bone pin

was their ability to absorb very varying peoples into their midst, and endow them with the Roman spirit. The great Trajan himself was a Spaniard. Fig. *70* shows the tombstone of a legionary, who, though he was born in Macedonia, lived and died in Lincoln. He may have had a British wife, and told his Romano-British children tales of what he did when he was a boy.

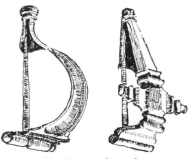

28 Bronze brooches

Having seen something of the people and their appearance, we can now pass to the Romano-British houses, and nowhere shall we find a better illustration of Roman skill. The Roman house of Italy was built round small courtyards to exclude the sun. The entrance from the street led into the first of these courtyards called the atrium, which was roofed over except for a central opening, the compluvium, above a shallow basin in the floor, the impluvium. There were small bedrooms at the sides of the atrium, and the tablinum, or reception-room, was opposite the entrance; this room also opened on to the peristyle at the back. This was the garden surrounded by colonnaded walks, at the far end of which, opposite the tablinum, was the exedra, which answered the same purpose as a modern drawing-room.

The Roman in Italy built his house around a courtyard, but in England he wisely realized that he could not afford to shut out the sun, and so opened up the whole plan. The so-called "villa" was really a large self-contained country establishment, with its farm outbuildings. A number have been discovered and excavated in the southern part of England, and among them we may mention as typical instances those at Lullingstone, Kent; Bignor, Sussex; Brading, Isle of Wight; North Leigh, Oxford-shire; and at Chedworth, Gloucester and Hambleden, near the Thames, where small museums have been built for the objects brought to light.

Fig. *29* shows the plan of a Roman villa, at Spoonley Wood,

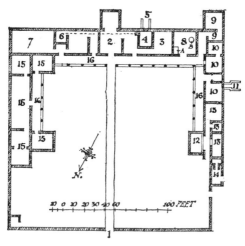

29 Plan of a Roman villa

well placed in a combe
opening off the main
escarpment of the
Cotswolds, near
Winchcombe, Glou-
cestershire.

Here we have the
entrance at 1 leading
into a large court-
yard, or combination
of atrium and peri-
style, and this leads,
as in the real Roman
house, to the tabli-
num at 2. The tricli-
nium, or dining-room,
was at 3, with a
specially heated room, for use in winter, at 4. As the
heat from the stoke-hole, 5, is taken under all the rooms
to 6, these appear to have been reception-rooms. Room
7 was not heated, so may have been a summer-room. The
kitchen was at 8, with larders and stores at 9. The three
rooms at 10 are heated from the stoke-hole at 11, and so must
have been for winter use, or for other branches of the family,
living under the same roof. Rooms 12 and 13 were the bath-
rooms cut off from the house, with their own separate entrance
from the courtyard. The three rooms, 13, were heated from a
stoke-hole at 14, and were the frigidarium, tepidarium, and
caldarium. At 12 was the cold bath, 16 feet by 11 feet 6 inches,
quite big enough for a plunge and kick about. Evidently
cleanliness ranked high as a virtue in Roman times; very much
higher than in the time about which Thackeray wrote in
Pendennis. Here the old Benchers in the Temple complained
bitterly about the water which was spilled on the stairs when
being carried up for Warrington's and Pendennis's baths; they
had always managed to do without baths, why did these
wretched youngsters want to go in for them? As Thackeray
points out, our ancestors, of not so long ago, were the "great
unwashed".

The slaves' quarters are supposed to have been at 15, without

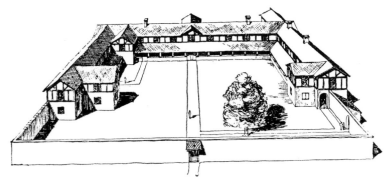

30   Exterior of a Roman villa

any communication with the house, except through the courtyard. So far as the form of the plan is concerned, there is not
any doubt at all; when we come to the structure which was
raised on it, we are on more debatable ground, and it may be
well for us to describe how we have built up the exterior shown
in fig. *30*. The colonnaded walks at 16 had dwarf columns
standing on low walls. We know this because the columns
which supported the roof were found at Spoonley Wood, 6½
inches diameter, and the Stonesfield slates with which it was
covered. This is shown in more detail on fig. *32*. The same
thing happened at Silchester. Here it was that a valuable clue
was gained as to the construction of the upper floors. In
excavating it was noticed that some of the ground floors were
covered to the depth of a few inches with a layer of clay, which,
on careful examination, showed marks of wattling. Wattle and

daub construction is
known to have been
used at the Glaston-
bury Lake Village, and
consisted of daubing
a mixture of clay and
chopped straw on to
wattle hurdles, fitted
in between timber
framing. It was
thought that the clay
on the floors at

31   Girls playing knuckle-bones

32   Courtyard of a Roman house

Silchester was the remains of a timber-framed upper storey that had decayed and fallen down. The appearance of the upper part of a Roman house would have been rather like mediaeval half-timbering, though our drawing looks more like a golf pavilion of today.

At Spoonley Wood, the ground-floor walls were built of local stone, and average 2 feet thick, and in almost all cases the walls of Roman houses were covered with stucco and coloured. At one of the houses recently excavated at Verulamium, it was possible to recover nearly a whole stucco wall in fragments.

These have been mounted on a stand and are now in the British Museum. The yellow stucco or plaster wall is covered with a most beautiful running scroll design decorated with beautifully painted peacocks. This gives us some idea of the fashion in interior decoration in Roman times.

Fig. 33 shows the Roman triclinium, or dining-room, and how the diners reclined on low couches round a centre table. It seems an uncomfortable method of feeding.

We referred on page 56 to the heated floors at Spoonley Wood. Fig. 34 shows how this was done, and it was a very clever method. If an architect today is designing an operating theatre in a hospital, he adopts the Roman way of heating the floors and walls, because it prevents the humid air from condensing on the walls, which it will do if they are cold. The Roman architect started with a layer of concrete at A; on this he placed large tiles at B, and built thereon square piers, or *pilæ*, C. On these were placed as caps square tiles at D, and others were bridged across at E; on this the concrete floor was formed, with its mosaic covering.

The stoke-hole was outside, and here a slave made the fire, which he may have pushed right under the floor, the degree of heat being settled by the amount of floor which could be reached

33   Roman triclinium or dining-room

34 Roman method of heating houses—by hypocaust

by the fire; if an ordinary room, for use in winter, was to be heated, then a duct from the furnace led to a central area, from which other ducts led to the vertical wall flues; if it was the caldarium, or hot room of a bath, then the whole floor was suspended over the heating space, and the wall flues were multiplied, and gathered into chimneys much in the modern way.

Fig. *34* can be used to describe the way the Romans decorated their rooms. The walls were plastered, and then painted in very joyous colours. At Reading Museum there are pieces of plaster found at Silchester, showing traces of vivid colour, and painted decoration; these seem to be based on imitations of marbles, and the effect, taken in conjunction with the mosaic floors, must have been very fine.

The floors of the houses at Silchester were finished in a variety of ways. In some mosaic was used. In others, the final coat was formed with a cement made of lime and small fragments of broken brick, which was rubbed down to a smooth surface, and then polished; this was called *opus signinum*. The mosaic floors were formed of small cubes, of differently coloured materials: black and orange sandstones, white and grey limestones, yellow and red bricks, and Purbeck marble. Fig. *39* shows the mosaic worker, cutting sawn sticks of these materials

35 Part of the Roman pavement found at Woodbridge, near Cirencester

36   Found at Wellow, Somerset, in 1737

37   Portion of tessellated pavement, found in Leadenhall Street,
London, in 1803

38   Found at Itchen Abbas, near Winchester, in 1878

ROMAN PAVEMENTS

into the cubes, or tesserae; he holds the stick on the top of a chisel, set in a wooden block, and cuts the cubes by tapping with the hammer, just as the old-fashioned sweetstuff man used to do. The hammer and chisel were found at Silchester. The commoner floors were laid with larger cubes. If an old Roman floor is examined, it will be found to have a pleasant hand-made appearance, whereas

39   Mosaic worker

modern mosaic looks like its imitation in oil-cloth.

Windows were glazed at Silchester, and the glass appears to have been cast in moulds, in the shape of the panes; it is just one more illustration of the fascination of History; here we are writing of window glass, and scientifically heated houses and, in a century or so, the fabric of civilization itself crumbles away, and we must wait until the thirteenth century before we find glass again in this country, and our twentieth-century houses are not yet so well heated. For artificial light, candlesticks were used, and lamps in which oil was burned (40).

We can now think of the very important detail of cooking, and in fig. 41 we see a gridiron, found at Silchester, and the method of using it. All cooking was done on a raised hearth

40   A lamp

made of masonry. One of these was found at Pompeii, with the pot in place, just as it was when destruction fell on the city. The charcoal used for fuel was kept in the arch below. The fire was

41 Roman kitchen

made on this open hearth, and the charcoal fumes, which are dangerous, must have been carried away by a hood over the hearth into a wall flue. We are indebted to a friend for an account of how cooking was carried on in a Florentine kitchen, as late as 1893; the same open hearth as shown in our illustration was used. In this were small holes about 9 to 12 inches square, and 6 inches deep, in which fires were lighted, and pots boiled in the ordinary way, or food was fried, or grilled. Many vegetable dishes were used or just the leg of a chicken fried in olive oil. It was when any baking had to be done that trouble arose, because the Italian seldom bakes, but prefers frying and boiling; they do not go in for making puddings, but buy them at the cake shop. When they had to bake, or warm up anything, they used a *Forno di Campagna*, or oven of the country, which consisted of a large round pan, like a saucepan, standing on legs; this was put over the fire, and a flat cover being placed on the pan, another small charcoal fire was made on the top, and the cook, with a fan, regulated the amount of heat. This somewhat resembles the old west-country method described in our book *Everyday Things in England* (Vol. I) and it may explain why it is that brick ovens are not found in the ruins of Roman houses in this country.

COOKING AND EATING

42   Samian bowl

The Romans in this country may have been like the Florentines of 1893, and not such great meat-eaters as the barbarians they conquered.

The cook shown in fig. *41* is making a sauce in a bronze skillet or saucepan, and a stew is simmering in the bronze cooking-pot. The large pots on the floor are used to keep oil and wine, and a flesh hook hangs from the end of the shelf. The oil-burning lamp was found at Newstead, a Roman fort near Melrose, in Scotland. On the table is a lipped vessel called a mortar, which had pieces of grit worked into the surface of the clay before it was fired, so that vege-tables and other food could be rubbed down in it. Corn continued to be ground into flour in mills as shown in *Prehistoric Times*.

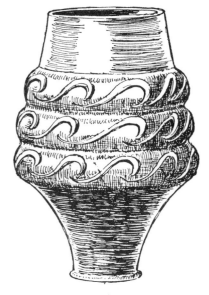

43   Castor ware

65

44   Decoration on Castor ware

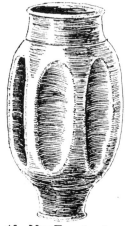

45   New Forest pottery

Food was sent up to the table in what is perhaps the most typical of all Roman pottery, the fine red glazed ware we call Samian, or *Terra sigillata*. This was made originally at Arezzo in Tuscany, and then spread through the Empire, and being copied by the potters of Gaul, was imported into Britain. The ornament was impressed from a mould. Fig. *42* shows a typical shape. There are, in the British Museum, many specimens of plain Samian ware, which have been dredged up from the Pudding-Pan Rock near Whitstable, Kent where they had been since the vessel which was bringing the pottery was wrecked in Roman times.

Castor ware (*43*) was made at Castor, near Peterborough, so it is a peculiarly British pottery. It appears to have been founded on Samian, but it is copper or slate colour, and the white ornament in low relief is not cast as the Samian, but executed with a pipe like the sugar decoration on a wedding cake. This ornament has a freedom which is Celtic

46   Roman glass

66

in its joyous curves. Fig. *44* shows a
hunting scene from another Castor
vase.

Very interesting pottery was made in
the New Forest(*45*); this was generally
reddish-brown or black.

Fig. *46* shows some typical specimens of Roman glass. As was the case
with the Samian ware of which we
have been writing, the glass was first
manufactured in the south of Gaul,
and then, in the second century, in
Belgium and at Cologne, and imported
into Britain. This stimulated the
British craftsmen, and it is thought
that the simpler types which are found
are their copies of the imported wares.
A visit should be paid to the Roman-
British Room at the British Museum,
where can be seen a most wonderful
pillar-moulded blue glass bowl. This
was discovered quite recently on the
Chiltern Hills, under a carriage drive.
The bowl was only a few inches below
the surface, and formed part of the fur-
nishings of a grave. By a miracle the

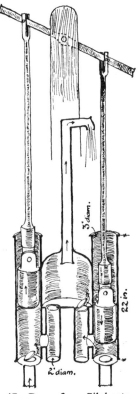

47   Pump from Silchester

pick made a small round hole through the bowl, but did not
crack it, so the Museum possesses the only complete bowl of
that kind of glass found as yet in England.

Fig. *47* shows how the householder at Silchester provided
himself with water. The drawing is a reconstruction of a force-
pump found there. The rocking arm worked the pistons, which,
moving up and down in their cylinders, sucked up the water
from the well underneath, through the valves as shown. The
descending piston shut one valve, and forced the water into the
central reservoir through the other, and so up to the discharge
pipe.

Great attention was paid to the details of sanitation. In
Crete, Sir Arthur Evans discovered an excellent system which
at a much earlier period made use of jointed drain-pipes; and

48   A Roman shop

underground sewers, flushed with water, were used by the Romans from a very early date.

From houses and home life, we can now turn to the trades and industries which supplied the inhabitants of Silchester with the everyday things they needed. The principal shops were in the forum, because this was the central meeting-place of the town, and they were very simply planned. The front was formed by a square opening in the wall(*48*). In this was placed the counter, built of masonry, with a gap at one end through which the shopman could pass, the customer preferring to stand on the pavement. A staircase led directly out of the shop to an upper room, and sometimes there was another room at the back of the shop. The shops were closed by wooden shutters, placed in grooves at top and bottom, and overlapping much as they used to do in England until the advent of roller blinds in recent times.

Today if you go into the back streets of an Italian city, or one of the smaller towns, you can find the shops still remaining much as we have described. In the larger places, alas, the hideous output of modern industry is very barely veiled behind plate-glass, as in our own London.

Fig. *49* illustrates an interesting pair of scales found at Silchester. The beam is of bronze, about 13 inches long, and graduated on the top, so that the instrument is a combination of steelyard and balance. Assuming that the fish being weighed is over 1 lb. in weight, a 1-lb. weight would be placed in the opposite pan, and another 1-lb. weight would be moved along the beam until the weight of the fish was balanced. If the fish were

49   Scales from Silchester

under 1-lb., then the 1-lb. weight would be placed in the opposite pan, and the other used on the beam, but this time on the same side as the fish. It was an extremely clever way of dispensing with many small weights.

50   The Roman steelyard

The steelyard works on the laws of leverage we explained in *Prehistoric Times*. These may be summarized in the diagram on fig. *50*. Imagine that these are the beams of steelyards; a 1-lb. weight 12 inches from the point of suspension will be balanced by a 2-lb. one on the other side 6 inches away; again, 1 lb. 12 inches away equals 4 lb. 3 inches away, and 1 lb. 12 inches away, equals 8 lb. only 1½ inches away. This will serve to explain the ingenuity of the Roman scale shown in fig. *50*. The leg of

51 A butcher's shop

lamb is hanging by hooks and chains to a ring with a moveable collar on the beam. If something heavier had to be weighed, the man held the scale by the middle hook, turned the beam round and brought another graduated scale into use; by our diagram we see that with the same weight of 1 lb. at 12 inches, he could weigh 4 lb. at 3 inches, or 8 lb. at 1½ inches. This is the reason for the three handles. The butcher shown in fig. *51* has a steelyard hanging up behind him, and while he cuts up the joints his wife enters the weights on a wax tablet with a stilus.

Interesting discoveries of tools were made at Silchester. In 1890, and again in 1900, when wells were being cleared out, hoards were discovered of very varying types. It is interesting to speculate how this came about. It is easy to understand how broken crockery, and other oddments, were found in wells and cesspools; a careless person would throw them down to get

52 Smiths and their tools

70

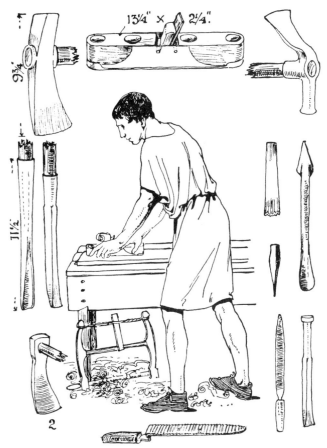

53   The carpenter and his tools

rid of them, but a careful workmen would not do this with good tools. In 1854, at Great Chesterford, Essex, another hoard was found, 6 feet deep in a pit, so it looks as if in the perilous times either at the end of the Roman occupation, or during the Saxon Terror, the workman buried his tools, hoping to be able to come back some day and start work again, and as he was not able to do so, there they have lain until discovered by the archaeologist of today.

The actual tools found at Silchester can be seen at Reading Museum, and so we are enabled to show the Roman at work.

71

54   Scythes and mower's anvil

Fig. *52* shows a smith using a pair of tongs which are quite modern in type. Besides making his own tools, he would have made those for other tradesmen.

The carpenter shown in fig. *53* has a metal-faced plane, 13½ inches long by 2½ inches broad, and was well provided with chisels, gouges, adzes, hammers, and axes; all the Silchester axes had hammer heads. He uses the same kind of saw as Italian carpenters of today. All the nails used would have been made by the smith. He made the mowers' anvils shown in fig. *54*; these were tapped into the ground, and used by men to temper the scythe with which they cut the corn. It is assumed that the strange-shaped implement the man is hammering, which

55   A shoemaker

72

56 A plough

was found at Great Chesterford, is a scythe; the one at the top
of the picture from Newstead is a better shape.

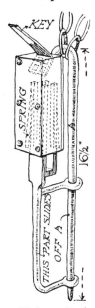

57 A padlock

The smith provided the iron last shown in
fig. 55, and with it the shoemaker mended
shoes as shown.

The smith, in fact, must have been a very
handy man; an adze was found(53, 2) with
a curved cutting edge, which suggests its
use by coopers to hollow the staves of
barrels. The coulter(56, A) helped the plough-
man, and points to an improvement on the
plough described by Virgil in the *Georgics*; this
consisted of a share beam to which was
attached the iron share, B, the shaft with a
yoke, and a vertical handle; not, in fact, very
much different from the primitive type shown
in *Prehistoric Times*. By the introduction of
the coulter a vertical cut was made in the soil,
and this could then be turned over far more
easily by the ploughshare. We have attempted
to show how we think the coulter was applied
to the plough of the Romans(56).

58 Handcuffs

The smith made large heavy padlocks of what seems to us an extraordinary pattern. Fig. 57 shows how these were operated. The key was inserted at the top into a slot, pushed into a vertical position, and was then forced down until it engaged with the four vertical rods shown by dotted lines. On the top of the rods were welded flat pieces of iron which were free to spring out at the bottom. The key was perforated to fit down over the ends of the rods, and being pushed down, compressed the flat springs, so that this portion could be drawn off A. We cannot say what the uses of the padlock were. At Great Chester-ford five handcuffs were found, attached to a smaller padlock of the same pattern (58); in the barracks of the gladiators at Pompeii, remains of stocks were found in the guard-room, which worked on much the same principle, so that here in England the padlocks were perhaps a means of discipline for slaves.

The Romans, being men of property, were quite used to locking up things. The simplest type of lock was one which had come down from Greek times, like the top sketch in fig. 59. Here a long key was pushed through a

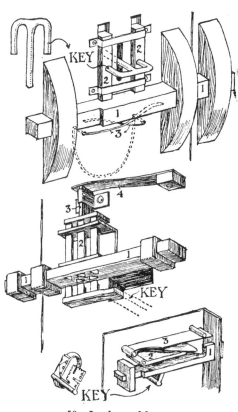

59 Locks and keys

vertical slot, then, being turned round, was hooked into two pegs or tumblers, 2, which being lifted up, allowed the bolt, 1, to be drawn back by a leather thong, 3, from the outside. In the centre sketch of fig. *59*, the pegs or tumblers, 2, are kept down into the bolt, 1, so that it is locked by a spring, 4; to unlock the bolt a key, rather like a tooth-brush at right angles to its handle, is placed under the bolt, so that the tumblers are pushed up, and the bolt can be drawn back by the key.

60 Money pot

The sketch at the bottom of fig. *59* shows how the tumbler type developed into the lever lock. The tumbler has become a projection on the underside of 2, which turns on a pin, and is kept in position by a spring at 3. The tumbler prevents the bolt, 1, being shot back by dropping into a slot in it. The key is inserted and turned, and levers up the tumbler. The key is interesting as it can be worn on the finger as a ring.

Fig. *60* shows how the Roman boy saved up his money in an earthenware pot that had to be broken before he could get at the contents.

In the north-west part of the town at Silchester, there appear to have been dyers' workshops. Here were found remains of furnaces, built rather in the same way as old-fashioned brick-set coppers. Woad and madder were used by the dyers. The woad plant was cut up and washed, partly dried, and ground up into a paste, and allowed to ferment. The paste was formed into balls, dried in the sun, and then being collected into heaps, fermented and became hot and fell into a powder. The roots of the madder plant were dried and ground into powder.

The fullers were important people with the Romans. First they had to deal with the new cloth. This was washed with fuller's earth, to remove the oily matter in the wool of which most of the clothes were made; it was then stretched to make it even, again washed to shrink it, carded to make the nap and, any inequalities being cut off, was finally pressed.

One of the fulleries at Pompeii has pictures showing the different processes. The white woollen cloth was bleached by

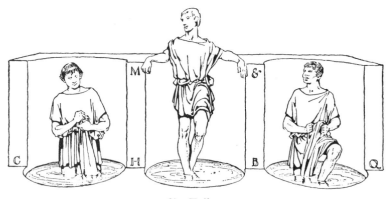

61 Fullers

being stretched over a frame, and subjected to the fumes of sulphur burning in a pot below. In fig. *8* a fuller is shown walking over the bridge into the town, carrying one of these bleaching-frames.

The fullers also dealt with the cleansing of dirty clothes. According to Mau, soap was a Gallic invention which had only begun to come into use at the time of the destruction of Pompeii, so in the pictures, to which we have referred, the fullers are shown at work doing the cleaning. The clothes were washed by being trodden in a vat by one man (*61*), while his next door neighbour did the rinsing. Fuller's earth would have been used instead of soap, and the clothes given careful drying and brushing before they were sent home again. Fig. *62* shows a fuller's assistant demonstrating how, by their process of cleaning, old clothes become

62 The fuller's assistant

76

as good as new. In St. Mark ix. 3, we read, "And his raiment became shining, exceeding white as snow; so as no fuller on earth can white them."

Vitruvius, in his tenth book, describes machines and engines, and it is obvious that the principle of the pulley was very well understood by the Romans. In a sepulchral relief of the Haterii, in the Lateran Museum, there is shown an excellent representation of a crane, and this we have used as the basis for our drawing (63). The power is here man-power, applied by a treadmill. Our drawing shows how the weight of the slaves would turn the wheels and so wind on to a drum between them the ropes, which, passing through pulleys, are attached to the stone to be lifted.

The tomb dates from the end of the first century, and is not so much a work of art, as an advertisement in stone of the doings of the family; the inclusion of the crane rather points to the Haterii as having been successful building contractors, or, perhaps, crane makers.

The crane would not have offered any great difficulty to the Roman in its making. Vitruvius describes a taximeter which, by an ingenious arrangement, dropped a pebble into a box for every mile of the journey, and a water-clock in which water dripping into a reservoir raised a float which turned the dial hands.

We may now pause to think how this trade and industry was carried on. Orders could not all have been given by word of mouth. A tile was found at Silchester which had scratched on it, FECIT TVBVL(um) CLEMENTINVS (Clementinus made this box-tile); another had SATIS (enough), and there were other graffiti, as these scratchings are called. These must be accepted as evidence that tile and brick-makers at Silchester knew how to write, and what is more, to do so in Latin. It is quite certain that the Romans did not import brickmakers, or that the Roman official made bricks for fun.

Another point to remember is that the Roman not only taught the Briton how to read and write, but he settled the form of our own letters. He took the alphabet of the Dorian Greeks, and gradually developed it into the form of the Trajan Column lettering (85). Inscriptions cut in stone, of this character, have been found in Great Britain. Examples can be seen in the

63 A crane

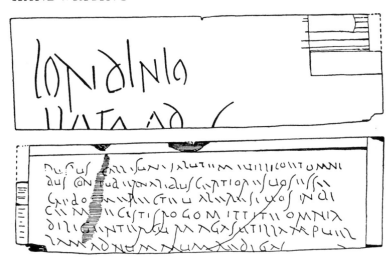

64   Roman writing-tablet from London

British Museum, and there is a very fine one on the front of a
Roman tomb found in Westminster Abbey, which has been
placed by the entrance to the Chapter House.

In writing we have the ordinary cursive, or handwriting,
which was used by the Silchester brickmakers in their scratchings
on the tiles, or by authors for their manuscripts. It is believed
that the shape of the letter in the Roman Cursive Script was
influenced by the fact that much of it was scratched, either
on metal, or more commonly with a small iron pointed pen
or stylus on wax-covered wooden tablets. This made it rather
angular, and it was just as varied as handwriting is today. Fig. *64*
shows a tablet found in Walbrook—a river in the City of London.
On the outside it has LONDINIO, and on the inside the
message, which we will give in Latin, line by line, so that you
can read the Roman Cursive Script in the illustration.

> Rufus callisuni salutem epillico et omni
> —bus contubernalibus certiores vos esse
> Credo me recte valere si vos indi
> —cem fecistis rogo mittite omnia
> diligenter cura agas ut illam puel
> —lam ad nummum redigas.

79

This is believed to be the longest cursive inscription in Britain, and this is how it reads in English.

> Rufus, son of Callisunus Greeting to Epillicus and all his fellows. I believe you know I am very well. If you have made the list please send. Look after everything carefully. See that you turn that slave girl into cash. . . .

The message is unfinished but it is quite plainly a business message from Rufus to his manager—from one Roman-Briton perhaps on a trading journey to Verulamium or farther off to another Roman-Briton with the address on the outside LONDINIO.

However, the scribes, who wrote out official decrees, or made fair copies of poems or histories, used what is called Bookhand, which, as one would expect, is more beautiful than the cursive we have been looking at. At first they employed a form of writing which consisted of what we should call capitals. From this they developed into what is called Uncial writing, where the forms were rounded, and so more suitable to the pen.

Finally these scripts passed out of use, and with the decline of Roman Britain we find the primitive Britain creeping back into the writing. Silchester here provides us with another illustration, and this time it is one which speaks of the city in its decay. A stone was found there with an Ogham inscription cut on it. Ogham writing is a very primitive arrangement of dots and dashes, which seems to have been invented in Ireland, and the Silchester inscription is thought to date from about the fifth century. This, coupled with the burying of tools we noted on page 70, enables us to draw a picture of the deserted town falling into decay. Here, where the brick makers at one time could scratch a Latin inscription on the wet clay of an unbaked tile, may have come, perhaps, a raiding Scot, whose only means of writing was this very primitive method.

65 Bronze figure from Silchester

66   Sacrifice

Having seen something of the trades and industries which
grew up around the Romano-British house, we can now turn
to the life lived therein, and see how the Roman fashioned his
soul. In one of the houses at Silchester an interesting discovery
was made of what is thought to have been the lararium or
chapel.

Roman religion centred around the house; there was the Lar,
or Lares, the spirit or spirits of the house, and a small bronze
statuette(65) found at Silchester, may have been one of these.
Cicero, in a speech of 57 B.C., said:

> Is there anything more hallowed, is there anything more closely
> hedged about with every kind of sanctity than the home of each
> individual citizen? Therein he has his altars, his hearth, his house-
> hold gods, his private worships, his rites and ceremonies.

Vesta was the spirit of the hearth, the Penates of the store
closet, and Janus of the door. The father was the Paterfamilias,
and acted as the priest, and his birthday was the festival of his
Genius, or inspiring spirit.

There were gods of the city and the Vestal Virgins guarded
the hearth fire of the State in their house by the Roman Forum,
and here Janus dwelt in the Gate. Jupiter was the God of
the sky, Juno of the Women, and Mars of War. The old
Nature worship had developed, until almost everything had its
spirit who must be propitiated by sacrifice. The spirits became

81

more tangible and the gods more heroic, but they were feared and not loved. Instead of the Christian belief that man is made in the image of God, the old gods were made like man. What the Roman wanted was the protection of the gods for the safety of his family and the prosperity of his city. For this he was prepared to pay a price, in the sacrifice of the first-fruits of his crops, or by the life of his ox, pig, and sheep; the god had the internal organs dedicated to him on the altar, and the flesh was eaten. What really counted was an elaborate ritual which had to be followed with great particularity. Fig. *66* is of a Roman sacrifice.

The Roman year was marked by a series of festivals at varying seasons—the Saturnalia, at sowing, from which many of our Christmas customs come; the Robigalia, for the aversion of mildew; the Ambarvalia, from which are derived Rogation-tide processions through the fields and the beating of bounds; and the Consualia at the harvest; and there were many others.

Augustus effected a great revival in Roman religion. It was about this time that we find the beginnings of Caesar worship, which became general, and was adopted for political reasons. Here it was not the man so much as his Genius which was worshipped.

As the Roman Empire extended, many Oriental cults were grafted on to the body of her religion, as those of Isis and Mithras. The latter seems to have appealed especially to the soldiers, and part of its ritual consisted of the novice being initiated by grades including physical and mental ordeals. Mithras was worshipped in underground temples, of which there is a very interesting example in the undermost of the three churches which form Ste. Clemente in Rome. There are traces of a temple on our Hadrian's Wall and another most interesting example of this curious underground religion was recently excavated at Walbrook in the City of London. The underground temple was in

67 Mithras

a wonderfully complete state of preservation, and the plan with seven pillars representing the seven grades of Mithraism and a sunken nave with raised side aisles in the Mithraic manner could easily be seen by the thousands who visited the site in the course of the excavation, attracted by this unusual happening in the middle of the busy London streets. Here too were found some splendid marble statues, some of them wearing the cap of Mithras like the figure in our illustration.

Apart from the soldiers' religions, which must have been derived from all parts of the Empire we also find traces of little domestic British cults. Among the Roman-British farmers in the South of England Hercules seems to have been very popular. The hill-figure of the Cerne Abbas Giant, interpreted as Hercules with his club, is believed to date from Roman times. Hercules may also be connected with the rural temples in Norfolk and Suffolk. One of these at Wilton in Norfolk, was recently found by accident while a farmer was ploughing up a field. It contained a crown of fine diadems (now in the British Museum) crudely cut out of sheet bronze and ornamented with single silver and bronze plaques stuck on with glue, and these have outline drawings hammered on them—a bearded face, a vase and two birds, a standing figure. This poorly made priest's "regalia" looks like the costume for a children's play.

Alongside the Wilton "Temple", which seems to have been a simple shed in a field, was another little hut containing a large collection of the little bronze safety pins of the sort which we have already illustrated. It seems in fact to have been a stall selling keep-sakes to the visitors to this wayside shrine. At Wilton we have come a long way from the Imperial Roman

68   Marriage

religion, but perhaps it gives us a truer picture of what the ordinary people believed in Roman times. And perhaps we are nearer here to the origins of Christianity in these islands. For Christianity began amongst very humble people.

We must now return to our discussion of Roman ceremonial.

Fig. *68* shows the solemn clasping of hands (*dextrarum iunctio*) which formed an important part in the Roman wedding. The *pronuba* or matron friend of the bride, stands behind the bride and bridegroom, and the man holds the marriage contract in his left hand. After this, prayers were offered to the gods and sacrifice made to Jupiter. The bride, on the night before, had put off her girl's clothes and dedicated them, with her toys, to the Lares of her father's house. On the wedding morn she wore the *tunica recta* with a woollen girdle, on her head was a chaplet of flowers, her veil was flame-like, and her shoes were saffron-coloured.

Our space will not permit us to write of the very interesting ceremonies which were observed at the birth of a Roman, or of all the festivals observed at the various seasons of the year. So we must pass on to the final stage of all—Death. We have in these books paid considerable attention to the methods of burial, and this must be done, because it is a detail in the lives of man that is very indicative of the "fashion of the soul".

As far back as the Mousterian Man of the Old Stone Age, we have found men burying their dead with varying ceremonial. In Roman times we find that burials, which were not allowed within the city walls, were placed instead along the roads leading to the town. At Silchester, Roman interments have been found at the side of the road leading to the North Gate. In early Roman times, burial was carried out by inhumation, that is by placing the body in a coffin in a grave dug in the earth. This may be by reason of their association with the Etruscans, who are thought to have been of Mediterranean stock, and so inclined to this method. Later, we find the Romans cremating or burning their dead, the ashes being disposed of in a variety of ways. Sometimes these were placed in glass jars, protected by being placed in leaden canisters; in other burials, pottery or marble urns were used for the same purpose. These were at times placed in graves, made in cist or boxlike form, of red

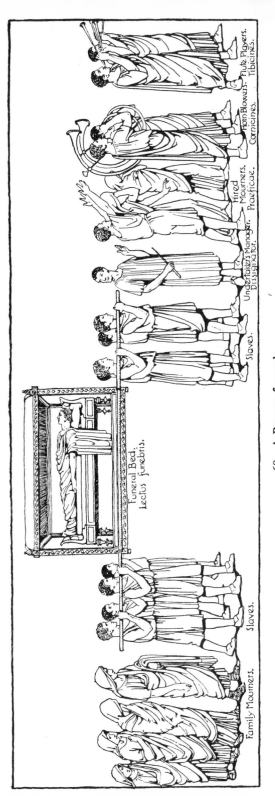

69   A Roman funeral

Flute Players.
Tibicines.

Horn-Blowers.
Cornicines.

Hired Mourners.
Praeficae.

Undertaker's Manager.
Dissignator.

Slaves.

Funeral Bed.
Lectus funebris.

Slaves.

Family Mourners.

tiles about 2 feet square by 3 inches thick. In these early cremations we find the old custom of burying articles for use in the spirit world: jugs, dishes, lamps, chairs, strigils, coins, mirrors, brooches, have all been found in England. As Christianity spread, this changed, and the soul of the Christian was not thought to need so many aids. Burial was once again by means of inhumation in coffins of wood, stone, or lead, the later ones lying east and west, with the head at the west. In modern times cremation has again been introduced.

70   A tombstone

Funeral ceremonies were elaborate in Roman times, and fig. 69 shows the burial of an important person of the time of Augustus. The dead body was laid out on the funeral bed in the house, and dressed in the toga. Torches burned at the corners of the bed, and there were hired mourners; money was placed in the mouth of the corpse, in Pagan times, to pay for the spirit's journey. The procession was headed by musicians, followed by the hired mourners, then came the funeral bed in its litter, followed by the family. A halt was made at the forum, and an oration delivered, and the procession would go to the place of burning outside the walls, where the body, being placed on a pyre, was reduced to ashes, which were collected and placed in an urn. Afterwards there was a funeral feast.

Fig. 70 shows the tombstone of Gaius Saufeius, who served for twenty-two years in the 9th Legion, and dying at the age of forty, was buried at Lincoln. The tombstone is now in the British Museum, in the gallery on the ground floor, opposite the emperor he served. The extended inscription is:

86

C(AIO) SAVFEIO
C(AII) F(ILIO) FAB(IA) HER(ACLEA)
MILITI LEGIO(NIS) VIIII
ANNOR(VM) XXXX STIP(ENDIORVM) XXII
H(IC) S(ITVS) E(ST)

From which we learn that Saufeius came from Heraclea in Macedonia, and belonged to the Fabian tribe; but there may be descendants of him in Lincoln today who have forgotten their ancestry.

Funeral monuments, as that of the Haterii, whence came the crane(63), afforded the Roman opportunities for the display of portrait busts. As we look at these today, it is easy to see that the portraits were speaking likenesses. It is interesting to note that with the advent of Christianity the dead were shown in attitudes of peaceful repose, until, with the coming of the Renaissance, they sit up and begin to take notice once more as in Roman times.

Chapter IV

THE ARMY, AND TRAVEL BY
LAND AND SEA

IT would be well worth going to Rome to see only the Column erected by Trajan to commemorate his victories over the Dacians. Here, in a sculptured band which ascends the shaft in a slow spiral, we see the Roman soldier at work. And his work is not only fighting; very much he appears to have been the handy man of the Empire, able to build a city, as well as to destroy one. If we cannot go to Rome, there is a first-rate plaster model of the Column at the Victoria and Albert Museum, South Kensington.

During the first three centuries of the Empire, the army was divided into legions and auxiliaries—the former being the descendants of the early citizens and farmers who left the plough to fight, and auxiliaries recruited from subject peoples. A legion was known by a number, and equalled about 5000 heavy infantry and 120 riders for dispatches and scouting. It was commanded by a senator, nominated by the Emperor as commander-in-chief (*Legatus Augusti legionis*), 6 military tribunes of high social rank, 60 centurions who equalled majors and captains and were promoted from the ranks, and other inferior officers. Legionaries served with the colours for twenty years, and received a bounty and land on discharge.

The auxiliaries were divided into infantry cohorts of 500 to 1000 strong, and cavalry troops (*alæ*). They were commanded by Roman officers, prefects, or tribunes, and while their pay was less, their service was longer than the legionaries; they received Roman citizenship on discharge.

The Emperor's Praetorian Guard was stationed in Rome, but the remainder of the army was on the frontiers; here the legions stopped, and were not moved about. They were grouped with auxiliaries, and commanded by the Governor of the Province.

The battles of the Empire were won by the legionary(*71*), who threw his javelin, and then rushed into close quarters and fought with his short sword (*gladius*), which was a cut-and-thrust weapon. The auxiliary cavalry operated on the wings, from which we get their name (*alæ*), and the Roman commanders do not appear to have wished to use them except in this way, thereby protecting the legionaries who delivered the main weight of the attack.

The tactics of this fighting at close quarters were to remain until the advent of the Martini-Henry rifle, issued to British troops in the 1870's which, by its longer range, removed the combatants from one another, and altered the whole strategy of fighting. The musket was not very much more effective, so far as range was concerned, than the longbow, and so long as it remained in use, the problem which confronted the soldier was the same as in Roman times—so to discipline your men that

71 A legionary

they would endure punishment until the psychological moment when the "knock-out" could be administered.

The pilum of the legionary(*71*) had an iron head fixed into a wooden shaft, and the weight of the iron head kept the javelin in a straight line when it was thrown. The killing range of the pilum was about thirty yards; compare this with the Tasmanian who could throw a wooden spear, nearly 12 feet long, and kill game at 40 to 50 yards. (See *Prehistoric Times*, page 52). The notes on fig. *71* will explain the remaining equipment of the legionary. Fig. *73* shows the scale armour of bronze tinned that was sometimes worn instead of the *lorica segmentata*, and fig. *74* the *caliga*, or sandal. Fig. *72* shows the equipment of the centurion. Fig. *75* is a belt buckle found at Newstead.

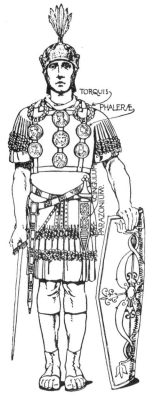

72 A centurion

Fig. *76* shows an auxiliary, who wore only a leather jerkin, without body armour, an oval shield, and a longer sword, the *spatha*(*78*). The auxiliaries who are shown on Trajan's Column wear the same dress whether fighting as cavalry or on foot. There were others as the slingers and stone-throwers(*77*); the archer(*79*); and the pioneer(*80*), using his *dolabra*, a combination of pick and axe.

The soldiers were rewarded for acts of bravery. The officer has phalerae on his breast, and torques

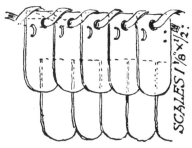

73 Scale armour (*Lorica squamata*)

74 Sandal (*caliga*)

taken from the neck of his enemy hang from his shoulders. Crowns were given as a reward: the *corona triumphalis* of bay for the *triumphator*; of oak leaves for saving the life of a comrade; in the form of a ship's prow for the first to board an enemy ship; as a city wall for the man who stormed the walls; as a rampart for those who

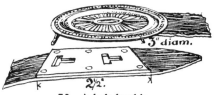

75 A belt buckle

90

took camps; and of plain gold for pure bravery.

The ensigns were carried by men with a head-dress made of a lion's or leopard's skin. These served to mark the maniples, or units, of which the legion was composed, and enabled the commanders to direct the movement of their men. Each legion carried the eagle, and to lose it was to ensure disgrace.

76   An auxiliary

The troops were accompanied by a medical corps. On Trajan's Column a wounded legionary is shown being assisted to a dressing-station, where an auxiliary is having his thigh bandaged in the modern way. At various points on the frontiers there were well-planned hospitals for sick troops.

The legionary was aided by effective artillery. Artillery is derived from a word which means to work with art, and doubtless the Roman did feel that his engines were works of art. They may have inherited the use of pro- jectile-throwing

77   Slingers and stone throwers

78 Swords

91

engines from the Greeks, but these appear to have been in general use in the Near East after about 400 B.C. Vitruvius the architect, writing about the time of Augustus, gives descriptions and elaborate formulae for the construction of catapultae, scorpions, and balistae for throwing javelins and stones. Catapultae are shown on the sculptures of the Trajan Column, and there is another on the tombstone, in the Vatican, of *C. Vedennius Moderatus*, who was an *architectus armamentarii* in the Imperial arsenal at the end of the first century A.D. From these sources there have been various reconstructions of these old engines, and those of Sir Ralph Payne-Gallwey, shown in his book, are of great interest, because he has made actual working models.

The first consideration of the Roman engineer was to remove his engine outside the range of the bow. This raises the question of the length of the bowshot. With the English longbow, the very longest range was 440 yards; but the archer of the Trajan Column(*79*) is shown armed with a bow of the Turkish pattern built up of horn and sinew, and there are accounts of shots of fabulous length with this. How-

ever that may be, the problem confronting the Roman engineer was not formidable, because it is obvious that the strength of the machine could very easily be made to exceed that of the man. Sir Ralph Payne-Gallwey succeeded in throwing a stone ball, 8 lb. in weight, from 450 to 500 yards, and he only depended on rope skeins for his power. The Greeks and Romans possessed the art of making these with hair and gut, but it was lost during the dark ages, and in mediae-val times the engineers de-pended on a counter-poised weight to throw the projectiles out of their trebuchets.

79   An archer

In classical times the power was obtained by torsion. Fig. *81* has been drawn from sculptures of the Trajan Column, and shows a catapult mounted on a small cart drawn by horses. The arms of the bow are composite, like the Turkish bow, and ends are fitted into the skeins of hair or gut. The ends of these skeins were passed through holes bored in the frame and then into large wooden washers. The skein was then secured by a pin through the centre, and was tightened by hand-spikes fitted into holes in the edge of the washer, and secured from springing back by catches, as shown. The skein was further tightened, when the bowstring was drawn back, by the winch at the end. This pulled back the carrier in which the javelin rested, and the bowstring being released, the heavy javelin flew off to come down into the besieged town. A variation of this engine for throwing stones was called the balista.

The onager in the same way depended for its power on a twisted skein, which in this case was horizontal. This skein was tightened in one way by hand-spikes as shown in fig. *82*, and in the other when the arm was pulled down by the windlass. This arm was built up to make it resist the shock of being stopped against the cross-piece of the frame. The stone ball, or rock, was placed in a leathern sling, and the trigger was a hook with an attachment by which it was pulled out of the ring on the arm. The stone ball, which was sent hurtling through the air, would have had sufficient force to crash through a roof.

The Romans also used the battering ram. In its simplest form, as shown on the Trajan Column, it consisted of a heavy beam which was carried by several men, and the point banged against the wall. After some few stones had been dislodged from the face, the rubble interior would not have presented so much difficulty to the breaching party.

Vitruvius gives descriptions of more elaborate forms, where the ram was suspended

80   An axe (Dolabra)

93

from the roof of a hut, made to run on wheels, and covered with raw hides, and as the machine moved slowly, it was called the tortoise of the ram.

Movable towers were brought into use so that the besiegers could approach the walls of a beleaguered city and fire into it at more advantage than from on the ground; other movable huts were contrived so that the ditches in front of the walls could be filled up, and the engineers, crossing on the causeway so formed, could undermine the walls.

The people of today who attempt reconstructions of these engines, are rather apt to provide their models with geared wheels enmeshed, the cogs of which could only have been cut on a machine; in our drawings we have suggested details which are much more home-made in character, and which the legionary could have made quite easily when he was far removed from his base; and we know, from the Trajan Column, that he was a very handy man.

Boys and girls will remember the dramatic part which catapults played in the destruction of Carthage. There was the mission of Cato to Carthage, in 157 B.C., from which he came back convinced that "Delenda est Carthago". Later, the Consuls, from their camp at Utica, demanded the surrender of all the Carthaginian weapons, and 200,000 sets of weapons, with 2000 catapults from the walls, were surrendered. Then came the final order, that Carthage was to be destroyed, and any new town that was built must be ten miles from the sea. It is one of the most tragic tales of history, how the Carthaginians, finding that they had been betrayed, seized on the scanty

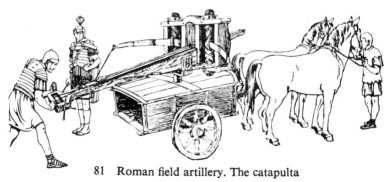

81   Roman field artillery. The catapulta

94

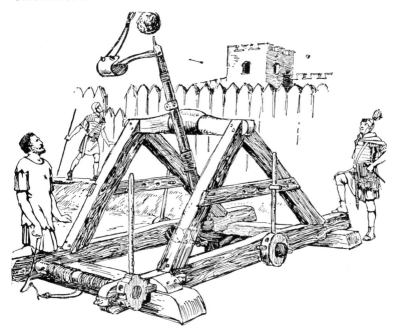

82   The onager

time which elapsed before the Romans started the siege, to
re-arm themselves; how new weapons and missiles were made
from the iron and lead of the buildings, and the women cut
off their hair to make skeins for new catapults. The Carthaginians, behind their walls, maintained themselves against all
the attempts of Scipio, until the last awful assault when the
Romans cut their way in, from wall to wall, through the houses,
to save the risks of fighting in the narrow streets. Then the last
scene of all, when the wife of Hasdrubal, cursing her husband
for his cowardly escape, killed her two sons, and perished with
their bodies in the flames. Then the site of the town was
obliterated by the plough and dedicated to the powers of the
Underworld. It was all typical of the tough Roman spirit which
would brook no rivals. If the drawings we have made of the
war engines serve no other purpose than to invest the tale of
Carthage with a new interest, and our readers with a determina-
tion to reconstruct on their own account, we shall be well
repaid for our trouble.

We can now leave fighting and find out how the legionary lived. The soldiers were quartered in forts, around which towns grew up; the legions occupied the larger fortresses at some distance from the frontier, as at York, where they could march out to the support of the auxiliaries who were manning the Wall. The country round supplied the cattle and corn.

The greatest relic of all is Hadrian's Wall, built across the neck of England from the mouth of the Tyne to the widening of the Solway Firth. The whole length was a little more than 76 miles. Though much is left of the Wall, it does not stand its full height anywhere; this is estimated to have been about 15 feet—the breadth in most places is $7\frac{1}{2}$ feet. Along the top there must have been an embattled parapet where sentries could walk, though this walk could not have been wide enough to form a fighting-platform. In fact, archaeologists do not regard the Wall as a military work, in the sense of one made to repel large forces, but as a fortified boundary line, a customs' barrier, definitely separating the Roman from the non-Roman territory.

The sentries who watched the Wall were housed in square towers, called mile-castles, which are separated a Roman mile apart from each other. At intervals, too, there were turrets which are believed to have been signal stations. We know a good deal more about Roman signal stations than we did even a few years ago, as a number of foundations of these which had not been noticed in the old days have been discovered and excavated. On the English shore of the Solway they extended for some way beyond the end of the Wall. The means of signalling is not known; but there is evidence for the use in the Roman world of visual signals including flags, semaphores, torches, flares and beacons. At longer intervals were placed great forts in which the garrisons lived, which supplied men for duty at the mile-castles, and where forces were always ready to stand to arms in case of emergency.

Beyond the Wall was a ditch of defence. Another ditch, known as the *Vallum*,[1] ran at a short distance from the near (that is, the Roman) side of the Wall. This puzzled the antiquarians for a long while, for it is unusual to have a ditch on the *inner* side

[1] The word "Vallum" means a mound and not a ditch. Originally there was a mound here on either side of the ditch. But in most places this has disappeared though the name is still attached to the ditch between the mounds.

83 Air view of the remains of the Roman Camp at Richborough

84 Hadrian's Wall climbing towards Winshields Crag, its highest point

SENATVSPOPVLVSQVEROMANVS
IMPCAESARIDIVINERVAEFNERVAE
TRAIANOAVGGERMDACICOPONTIF
MAXIMOTRIBPOTEXVIIIMPVICOSVIPP
ADDECLARANDVMQVANTAEALTITVDINIS
MONSETLOCVSTAN̄   IBVSSITEGESTVS

85 The Trajan Inscription

of a fortification. And the Vallum is not immediately next the Wall. Between them runs a military road to provide a means of communication and quick movement between points all along the line. But the mystery of the Vallum has now been cleared up. Its purpose was to prevent unauthorized civilians, not enemies, from approaching the military works of the wall. In places the line of the Wall passes over a tract of volcanic basalt—the hardest rock we have. Yet, in spite of this, the Vallum has been arduously cleft out and faithfully follows its course. When, at the present day, you look down on the ground and see the very groove which the Romans themselves had scored to mark the farthest limit of their sway, it will be strange if you feel no thrill, no shock, no mental dizziness. For there is something so simple and positive about that mark that it seems to knit the past right up to us in a way that no ruin of masonry can. And then, while we may feel almost in touch with the times of Hadrian, the contrast of what was, and what is, strikes us from another angle, but still underlined by the Vallum.

For if, when we look at the Vallum, we are Roman-minded, we feel ourselves to be standing at the farthest edge of civilization, cut off from the mainland by a belt of sea—from that mainland on which, two thousand miles away, stands our metropolis, the chief city of the world. But, if we suddenly turn twentieth-century-minded, what a transformation of geography! Our metropolis is close at hand; it is on the same island; as the greatest city of the world it has taken the place of Rome. It is not on the fringe of an empire but at the heart of one. How much greater is this privilege of citizenship! Yet, we may ask ourselves, if that line had not been drawn in the rock from sea to sea, if the Romans had not founded their Londinium for us to build our London on, would it ever have been our turn to take so great and responsible a place in the history of the world?

In this same history, the Vallum is like one of those marks on the jamb of a door which records the annual growth of the youngsters of a family. By it we may see where Rome grew to her full stature. As a nation and an empire we have made our marks in other doorways. But the family is not yet grown-up. When it is, it will cease to mark individual statures, Perhaps the time is nearly at hand.

But there is another aspect to the Wall. In spite of its strength and the grandeur of its masonry and that of all the buildings connected with it, it is really a monument to failure and not success. When that pillar of triumph, whose foundations we have seen at Richborough, was raised there was no thought of a fortified partition in Britain. It was taken for granted that, although Agricola could not be left to consolidate the country he had marched over, his successor would complete that task. Even when it was found necessary to build Hadrian's Wall hopes of subduing the rest of the country were still confidently entertained. An important stage in this direction was the building of another wall between the Clyde and the Forth. This one, made of turf instead of stone, was constructed by Lollius Urbicus, who was Governor of Britain in the time of Antonius Pius. Under the name of the Antonine Wall, its ruins still remain. But it could not be held. It was too late. The Roman Empire was decaying. Instead, much work was continually put into the upkeep and repairs of Hadrian's Wall, which one must therefore regard as a monumental admission of defeat.

There were some sixteen large forts in connection with the Wall, and at more frequent intervals, smaller forts (mile-castles) and turrets.

As the Roman fort was just as carefully planned as the Roman town, it may be as well to describe it here. The fort followed the same lines as the camp. When the legion was on active service and camped for the night, it did so behind earthen walls of a regular pattern. Polybius has left a description of the Republican Camp, and Hyginus of that of the Empire (86). The praetorium, where the tent of the commander was pitched, formed the centre of the camp, and around it were grouped the quarters of staff and bodyguard. At the back was a forum where the soldiers could meet, and again behind this the quaestorium, or paymaster's office. The Roman forts were provided with granaries to hold sufficient corn for a year, so that they could withstand siege. Tribute was based on property

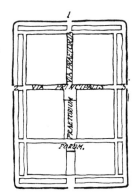

86   Roman camp described by Hyginus

and a corn tax which went to feed the army. The forts were provided as well with baths. The street in front of the praetorium was the Via Praetoria, and led to the Porta Praetoria, 1. The street which went across the camp was the Via Principalis, and led from the Porta Principalis Sinistra, 2, on one side, to the Porta Principalis Dextra, 3, on the other. The tents of the legionaries and their auxiliaries were pitched in the vacant spaces between these. When a fort had to be built, as at Newstead near Melrose, or on the Wall, the soldiers quite naturally built it in the form of the camp to which they were accustomed.

Wherever the Romans went they carried with them their love of the games, and here we would remind our readers that we shall obtain a very false perspective of history if we take our viewpoint from too modern an angle. We think of the doings of the Spanish Inquisition with horror, but Torquemada and Co. only adopted the usual methods of the secular courts of their time, the rack, pulley, and bucket of water, in their attempt to cure souls. In the same way we must remember that the *Meditations* of Marcus Aurelius, which have comforted many men since, were written by a man who must have attended the games. Originally these had formed part of religious ceremonies, and gladiators first appeared in the funeral games.

We have seen that there was an amphitheatre at Silchester (6), and there was another at Dorchester(87). Compared with the Colosseum, for example, these are simple constructions of

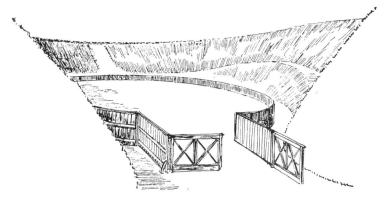

87 The amphitheatre at Dorchester

88   A Samnite
gladiator

earthen banks, but the displays given would have been much the same as those of Rome, though less elaborate.

Castor ware, which we have seen was an entirely British pottery, is sometimes decorated with gladiatorial combats. There is an ivory statuette of a gladiator in the British Museum, of the same type as shown in fig. *88*, and gladiators are shown in mosaic work at Bignor, Sussex. Beyond this we cannot go, and our readers if they like can people the amphitheatre we have shown. They can imagine the parade, and then the sham fight with blunt weapons, to be followed by the real thing.

The gladiator (*88*) might not have to fight against another armed in the same way, but could have been matched against the *retiarius*, armed with net, trident, and dagger. If the men held back, they were thrashed into the fight with whips. There must have been wary feints, and lunges, and then a slip, when the net was cast, and the fallen man was hopeless in its entangling folds; but not perhaps quite hopeless, because if he had fought well, he could appeal to the spectators, and be granted reprieve if they waved their handkerchiefs; but if the thumbs were turned down then all that remained to the poor gladiator was one glance to where the bearers stood waiting with the bier for his dead body, before the dagger found a vulnerable spot, and his blood stained the sand. This may have happened at Silchester.

Fig. *89* has been drawn from the Ribchester helmet in the

89   Vizor helmet

102

British Museum. This is made of thin bronze, and has a vizor modelled in the form of a face. An iron helmet of the same pattern was found at Newstead, and another of brass. It is thought that these helmets were used by the Celtic auxiliaries in their games.

Mr. Curle, in his book on Newstead, gives an account of the sports and exercises indulged in by the Roman cavalry in the time of Hadrian. From this we find that the vizor helmets were used by the men when taking part in a tournament, and were crested with yellow plumes; they carried gaily decorated shields and wore tunics, sometimes scarlet, or purple, and at others parti-coloured. Their horses were protected by frontlets and trappings from the showers of wooden spears which were discharged in the sham fights. Here is a pleasant picture of the legionaries grouped around the lists, into which ride these very gorgeous horsemen, to go through their evolutions; it was not all work in remote Newstead.

Having dealt with the Army and its bearing on British history, we can turn to the Navy, and just as the Roman generals did not rely on cavalry, so the Empire depended rather on the legionary than on sea-power. The Roman Navy seems to have been used more for the purposes of transport than as an effective fighting force.

When we come to the Roman ship, we find that there is not much more known about it than the Greek trireme; the writers were not sailors; the sculptors thought more of the design of

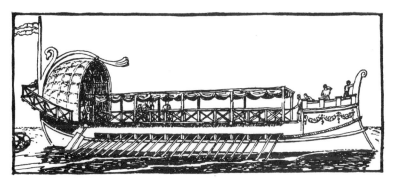

90   Roman galley

103

91   A Roman merchant ship

their sculptures than the detail of the ships they were carving, and the sailors who did know, neither wrote, nor drew. Fig. 90, of a Roman galley, is based on those shown on Trajan's Column. The prow is carried up in forecastle fashion, and at the stern is a tilt. There are paintings at Pompeii showing galleys fitted with a mast and a square sail.

Fig. 91 is of a Roman merchant ship, and here again we have gone to the Trajan Column sculptures, assisted by Professor Sottas' article in the Mariner's Mirror, on "The Ship of St. Paul's Last Voyage". This took place in A.D. 60, and is described by St. Luke in the 27th chapter of the Acts of the Apostles. This description is valuable, as showing the sizes, and general details, of the Roman ship at about the time when Britain was coming under the influence of Rome. We find that when the ship was caught in the easterly gale "we had much work to come by the boat", which had been in tow, and had to be hoisted on board; by "undergirding the ship" with ropes they added to its powers of resistance; they lightened the ship, "and the third day we cast out with our own hands the tackling of the ship". "When the fourteenth night was come" the water shoaled rapidly from 20 to 15 fathoms, so that "they cast four anchors out of the stern".

The sailors were made of poor stuff, because they were "about to flee out of the ship, when they had let down the boat into the sea, under colour as though they would have cast anchors out of the foreship". We find that there were "in all in the ship two hundred threescore and sixteen souls".

Professor Sottas, in his article in the *Mariner's Mirror*, illustrates a model which he made of St. Paul's ship, based on the carving of a merchantman on a tomb at Pompeii, and another from Ostia, and these have many points of similarity with that of the ship on the Trajan Column. From these sources we find that the merchantman, or round ship, depended on its sails, and did not have oars like the galley; there was a tilt at the stern, with a gallery outside it, and another at the prow, with the crew's quarters behind in the forecastle. The mainsail and foresail were brailed up in a peculiar way, the sails were divided up into squares, with leather strips, having eyes at the intersections, and through these ropes were passed, and the sail drawn up rather like a blind.

Now we come to one of the facts which, we think, illustrates what the Roman occupation meant to this country—the *pharos*, or lighthouse, which they built at Dover. The foundations still remain, and in fig. *92* we show a galley which has made the cross-channel trip at night, and reached the land safely. During the Middle Ages, the lighting of the coasts was regarded as an act of piety, and a few lights were maintained on church towers, but it was not until well on in the nineteenth century that any real progress was made. Here, as in so many other ways, the Romans anticipated what was necessary in a civilized state.

If we leave our ship on the coast, we need roads to travel by on land, and this was an especial need for the Romans with their huge Empire to administer. By the roads were conveyed to and from Rome the official post and documents by which this administration was carried out. We are all of us far too ready to take things for granted; we walk on a Roman road, and are not thrilled; we may say, "Well, after all, it is only a road", and we forget the travellers who through all the centuries, have hurried along its surface. It is interesting to speculate why a road

92   A Roman lighthouse

should be in the position we find it. The answer, that it serves to connect two towns, may not contain the whole essence of the matter, because we can then ask why the towns have grown up in these places. There must be certain ways up and down a country, but these would not be very useful unless they connected areas where men could grow corn, or rear cattle, or find iron and coal with which to work.

Though there were 2000 years of farming in Britain before the Romans came very little headway could have been made in clearing the land permanently for cultivation. We forget today what constant effort is needed to hold Nature in check, but a reminder can be seen at the Rothamstead Experimental Station, Harpenden, Hertfordshire. Here, some years ago, it was determined to leave untouched a piece of arable land and see what would happen. Gradually the weeds took possession, then bushes, and now large trees give the land the appearance of forests.

If we are motoring along a Roman road, it is noticeable that it goes in as straight a line as possible between the towns it connects, but if it is necessary to alter the direction this is done on high ground. This is thought to prove that the surveyors who laid out the roads in Roman times, did so by fires lighted on the hilltops. It would then be quite a simple matter to set out the intermediate points, sighting the flames by night or the smoke by day.

We may, in fact, think of the Roman roads as preparing us for our advancement in two ways. The most obvious of these is the ease which they enabled us to move from one part of the country to another. But this ease of locomotion brought another blessing with it. The roads, once established with their forts and strong-points, opened trade routes and founded trade-centres. Although the power of Rome declined, and her buildings fell into utter dilapidation and decay, the roads held out—in spite of neglect. They fostered the life-blood of the new civilization until the coming of the railways. When the railways were made, the centres of business and the market-towns were ready to make the most of the new form of transport, for *the roads had made the towns*. We, in our time, have seen the process reversed again. For now, since the coming of the motor, the towns make the roads.

107

But while many new arterial systems have come into use, from Telford's time to our own, the Roman roads are still the main thoroughfares both for touring-car and heavy vehicle. From Dover to London; from London to Norwich, to Newcastle, to Chester; from Chester to Carlisle; across the wild tops of the Pennines the oil-driven rubbered wheel circulates our civilization over the work of the Roman engineer.

Yet there is one great Roman road which has not, and never has had, any continuous mission for commerce, that is the Fosse Way. It is the straightest of the Roman roads and goes from Axminster, near the south coast, to Lincoln, near the shore of the North Sea, with no more than six miles out of the same straight direction. Most of it is still to be traced, and it is only used in places as a modern road. The truth about it is that it was never intended to be used as a commercial highway at all. It was made after the first phase of the Conquest was completed—just after the first half of the first century. It was made as a military road, and something more than that. You may compare it with the Vallum at Hadrian's Wall, for it was constructed to indicate where the frontier of the Roman Empire rested after the south-east of England had been annexed and the first phase of conquest completed.

The Fosse Way is also of great interest in showing what an amazing grasp the Romans had of the life of the land when they had only been here for three or four years. They naturally had no maps; the country, up to a considerable altitude, was covered with dense forests; the inhabitants were hostile. Yet they mastered a fact of our physical geography which many well-educated people who have lived in England all their lives are unaware of. They realized that there was a natural division which parted England into two main masses, and that it lay along the north fringe of the Cotswold Hills, along the lower Severn Valley, and then up towards the springs of the Avon. Here stands the watershed. Beyond are the springs of the Soar; and the Soar Valley leads into the Trent Valley, which goes on in a direct line to the Humber and the salt water of the North Sea. The Fosse Way occupies the south side of this important division and, for the most part, does so in such a way as to command the country to the north-west.

The next powerful thrust was bent against Wales and no

108

doubt went forward along the lines of what came, in later times, to be known as the Watling Street. This road, which is still in service for the whole of its length between Wroxeter (near Shrewsbury) and London, crosses the Fosse Way at the very point which we—having before us a physical map of Britain done in colours carefully and competently by H.M. Ordnance Survey—should have suggested ourselves. It crosses at the watershed, that small area which separates the waters of the basins of Severn and Trent. The place is called High Cross (*Venonæ* was the name of the Roman station), and is well marked by a peculiar Georgian milestone which takes the form of a small monument. From here the Watling Street takes a slight swerve to the west and ends its Roman course at Viroconium, now known as Wroxeter.

When they came to the construction of the roads, the Romans very properly used local materials: stone in a stone country, and flint and gravel where these were found. It is a mistake to think that the Roman road was always paved with stone, but one outstanding feature is that the road was almost invariably raised up on a causeway. The country was not so well drained as it is today, and so the causeway would have kept the road dry in the bottoms, yet the Romans would repeat it over the top of a chalk Down.

On our map(*1*) we have given an outline of what the principal authorities accept as the Roman road system.

Fig. *93* is of the milestone in the Roman Sculpture Gallery at the British Museum. The Roman mile was 1617 yards in length, and this stone was set up 8 miles from Kanovium (Caerhyn, near Conway). The Latin inscription is as follows:

93   A Roman milestone

109

IMP . CAES . TRAI
ANVS . HADRIANVS
AVG . P . M . TR . P
. P . P . COS . III .
A . KANOVIO
. M . P . VIII .

This they would have extended to IMPERATOR CÆSAR
TRAIANVS HADRIANVS AVGVSTVS, PONTIFEX
MAXIMVS, TRIBVNICIA POTESTATE. . . . . PATER
PATRIÆ, CONSVL III, A KANOVIO MILLIA PASSVVM
VIII. The *British Museum Guide* points out that these are the
titles of the Emperor Hadrian, and his third consulate dated
from 119, but as the year of his tribunician power is uncertain,
the inscription can only be dated between A.D. 119 and 138.

It must be remembered that our Roman roads were only a
part of the system which radiated all over the Empire. Augustus
set up a Golden Milestone in the forum at Rome, on which
the distances to the principal cities of the Empire were given.
He also set up a regular state post by which dispatches could
be carried.

The Romans used various types of vehicles. There was the
lectica, or litter, like the eighteenth-century sedan chair; the
ræda, a four-wheeled waggon used when a number of people
wanted to travel or luggage had to be carried. For faster

94 A racing chariot

110

travelling there were two-wheeled carts covered with a tilt and drawn by a mule.

Fig. *94* shows a pair-horse chariot which would have been used for racing or as a sporting conveyance. The bridle bit(*95*) was found at Newstead, and fig. *96* is of what is called a hipposandal, at the British Museum. Ordinary horse-shoes were known to the Romans, but smiths may have been few and far between. These hipposandals may have been used to tie on to the horses' hoofs as shoes

95 A bridle bit from Newstead

when the farmer wanted to take his horses on to the hard roads, in much the same way as a horse wears shoes to prevent his feet cutting the turf when pulling a mowing machine.

As the history of Roman Britain depends largely on the Roman soldier, we can sketch it in very briefly here. The invasion of 43 was carried out by four legions and auxiliaries, in all probably about 40,000 men, and before the death of Claudius, the Romans had progressed as far west as Exeter, and Shrewsbury, and up to the Humber. From that time to the building of the Wall by Hadrian to define the northern frontier, was the period of conquest, the principal dates of which are noted in the Chronology.

The Romans penetrated into Scotland as early as the time of Agricola, but the north of Britain never passed out of the soldiers' hands, and few towns or villas were built to the north of York, or beyond Shrewsbury and Exeter. The Second Legion

96 A hipposandal

111

was stationed at Caerleon, near Chepstow; the Twentieth at Chester, and the Ninth, and later the Sixth, at York. It is interesting to think of Britain as being the north-west Province of the Roman Empire, and needing as careful guarding as India in more recent times.

Britain must have owed a great deal to the wise government of Agricola, of whom we hear in the writings of his son-in-law Tacitus. It is probably during this period, A.D. 78–85, that Silchester, Bath, and Caerwent were commenced, and Latin began to be spoken, and the toga worn.

During the second century there were serious risings in the North, but the country on the whole was enjoying peace, and during the third century must have been very prosperous; after that began signs of the great upheaval which in the end was to overwhelm Rome. The English became troublesome as early as A.D. 300 when the Saxon shore was fortified against them. This was done by a series of forts built round the coast from the Wash to Portsmouth. The ruins of many of these remain today, and one of the most interesting is that at Portchester. Here the Roman walls enclose a Norman church and castle keep which has later Gothic additions. From the old ramparts one looks out over the water of Portsmouth Harbour to the Royal Dockyard due south. So here in this one little spot is some 1100 years of architecture, and the docks, with the forts on the hills behind, are a reminder that watch and ward has been kept for over 1600 years.

Portchester is the best of the Saxon shore forts. It is practically complete with its wall-walks and its bastions, embracing the immense area of nine acres. The next best are Richborough, Pevensey in Sussex, and Burgh Castle at Yarmouth. There are relics at Reculver (the far end of the sea channel between Thanet and the mainland, of which Richborough was the southern entrance), and at Lympne, on Romney Marsh. Remains of the Roman fort at Dover are not so certain, but the lighthouse already mentioned (page 105), still stands. Less known is the single example on the west coast of the same type of fort as those of the Saxon shore. This is to be seen at Holyhead. The parish church stands within the enclosure.

At Richborough in Kent, one of the best known of these Saxon shore forts, we have a complete picture as to how things

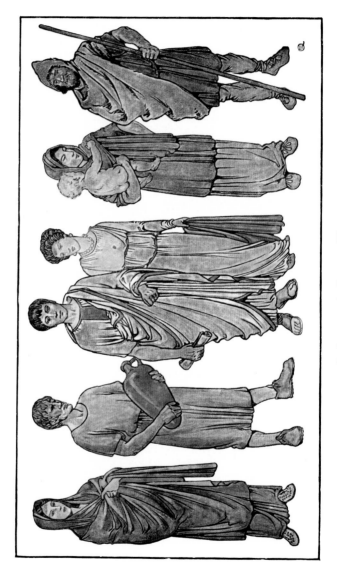

97 Costume in Roman Times

went from the beginning of the Roman occupation to the end of it. In the old days, there was a narrow sea passage between the mainland of Kent and the Isle of Thanet. It was at the south end of this—opening on to the Straits of Dover—that Richborough was situated. The invading legions which came over in the year 43 (page 111) landed here and threw up a double ditch and palisade to secure their first footing in our country. The actual remains of this can now be seen at Richborough since excavation has made it plain.

Near by, stands a mysterious cross-shaped mass of masonry which goes far down into the ground and is solid throughout. It is still something of a riddle, though perhaps more than half the answer has been guessed; for the fine detective work of the archaeologists has shown it to have been the foundation of an immense monument, the like of which was not raised in any other part of Britain by the Romans. That part of the riddle which remains unsolved relates to the purpose of this monument. But it is a fair guess that it was raised after the triumphs of Agricola to the conquest of the whole of Britain. At that time the major part of the work had been done, and it was thought the rest would be child's play. But Agricola was ordered to go and fight in another part of the Empire at the critical moment. And when matters were taken in hand again it was too late. Britain was never entirely conquered. The advanced wall, built beyond Hadrian's, between the inlets of Firth and Clyde, could not be held; and Scotland and Ireland remained till the end outside the boundary of the Roman Empire.

In the days when the monument was erected, Richborough was undefended. There seemed to be no need to defend it, for the English Channel was within the bounds of the Empire. But the name of Rome began to grow less awe-inspiring to the men who lived in the uncivilized "outside" world, for political greed and struggles for power had weakened the spirit and the force of the nation. Macaulay writes as one who lived at that time when he says:

> Now Roman is to Roman
> More hateful than a foe,
> And the Tribunes beard the high,
> And the Fathers grind the low.

THE ARMY, AND TRAVEL BY LAND AND SEA

As we wax hot in faction,
In battle we wax cold;
Wherefore men fight not as they fought
In the brave days of old.

So the Barbarians grew bold, and took to the sea in raiding parties—Saxons from north of the Roman Empire's boundary in Germany and the men of the un-Romanized isle of Ireland, called at that early time the Scots. At Richborough, this time of fear, which was shortly after the year 250, is vividly illustrated by two rows of banks and ditches cast round the old landing-place (with the monument at its centre). It had been found necessary to defend the entrance to Britain. On the air-photograph (*83*) these entrenchments are clearly seen. But if the picture is studied it will be seen that that is not the end of the story. The defences were probably thought of as a temporary measure to stave off trouble until such time as Rome had reasserted herself, and come back into her old and proper glory. But the barbarian pirates, far from becoming quelled, grew more daring and more dangerous; and Rome, which had once relied on prestige for defending these open waters, had now to come down to the more humiliating device of building local castles at the worst danger points. Thus, towards the end of the third century were built the immense stone walls of the fort at Richborough, which have remained to our own time, and are seen in an air-photograph standing four-square round the works in earth and masonry, which mark the earlier stages of the Roman occupation of the country.

These walls are associated with a very dashing and picturesque character, the admiral Carausius, who made himself emperor by stealing his own fleet, and who struck such a number of penny pieces that they are among the commonest of the Roman coins which you may pick up anywhere in Britain. There is no room here to go into details of the adventures and career of Carausius, interesting as they are, but there is a significant thing to be noted about the building of the walls before we pass on from Richborough. Among the materials which have gone into their making are a number of pieces that can be said with certainty to have come from the structure which stood on the cross-shaped base and was, we guess, a monument to mark the triumph of the Roman arms in Britain. That fragments of this

116

98 The Great Dish

99 A Pair of Platters

THE MILDENHALL TREASURE

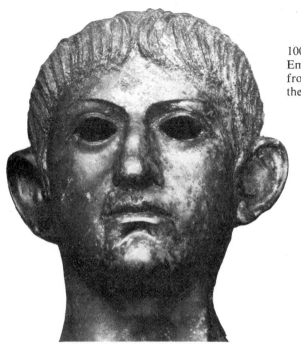

100 Bronze head of the Emperor Claudius. Loot from Colchester found in the River Alde, Suffolk

101 Roman Tombstone, Hexham Abbey

102 Roman Altar, Caerwent

should be built into the walls raised nearly two and a half centuries after the time of Agricola, shows, first of all, that the monument must, even at that date, have been neglected and in ruins; and secondly, that it was no longer regarded as a thing to be proud of. Perhaps its presence was even felt to mock the Romans of that day and to commemorate failure rather then victory.

There were migrations of Celts, from Ireland to Caledonia, who were oddly enough called, not Irish, but Scotti. The Picts became troublesome about 343, and with the Scotti raided into England. Men began to bury their tools and treasures, as we have seen on page 71, and when hoards of coins are found, they are not, as a rule, dated later than 350–360. The most famous buried find is that of the Mildenhall Silver Treasure from which we illustrate some pieces (98–9). This was found in Suffolk in 1946. The dishes and bowls had been carefully buried in the troubles at the end of the fourth century, and are still in beautiful condition after all this time. The treasure contains goblets, spoons, and bowls as well as the beautiful platters and dishes which we illustrate. One still feels sad for the Romans who buried them so carefully in time of trouble and never returned to collect them.

It was about this time that the army was remodelled, and made more mobile, to meet the attacks of the Barbarians, with light troops, and more cavalry. The Governors were not trustworthy, and there were Dukes of Britain, Counts of Britain, and Counts of the Saxon shore, in case one alone should aspire to be Emperor.

Now we must not think of Britain all this time as having been occupied by a very large number of Romans who kept the British in subjection. As the latter settled down to Roman rule, the true Romans could not have been more than the official classes, and the skeleton of the army. We must imagine the more experienced of these being gradually recalled as the pressure on Rome increased. Many of the Britons were citizens of Rome, and looked on themselves as Romans; they did not stand on the cliffs at Dover, as the last boatload of Romans left, and cheer, thinking they had seen the last of their enemies. By this time they regarded themselves as Romans, and her enemies were theirs, and very terrible ones too.

The trouble started with a great stirring up of the peoples of the Central Asian plains. Driven perhaps by drought, the fierce and warlike Huns surged towards the Goths, whom they defeated. The vanquished moved across the Danube and Rhine, and, with the Huns behind them, were forced into the Roman Empire. Rome was captured and sacked in 410, and the movement was not stopped until Attila, the King of the Huns, was defeated at Châlons in 451. By this time the elaborate organization of the Empire had broken down, and Europe had entered into the Dark Ages.

Here in Britain we can imagine the Britons holding their own as best they could against their enemies, but being gradually forced into the west, where they joined up with the Celts, and settled down in a primitive environment. Those who did not fly would have been killed, or sold into slavery. The Jutes, the Angles, and Saxons must have come up to a deserted Silchester, and have gaped at its wonders, as something entirely outside the range of their understanding. Britain and Europe were to wait for a thousand years before the ideas which Silchester expressed again became the thought of the day.

Chapter V

THE COMING OF THE ENGLISH

THE collapse of Roman rule in Britain was a gradual process and the incursions of those people we know as Anglo-Saxons took place over a long period of time. The Roman army and the Roman civil service officially withdrew from Britain about the year 410, but traces of Roman government and administration survived for many years after this: gradually, however, Roman civilization was forgotten, the towns were abandoned and the straight Roman roads fell into decay. At Silchester an intruder penetrated one of the many deserted houses of the Roman town and camped there for a short time, lighting a fire in the middle of the mosaic floor. Neglect was the chief cause of the downfall of Roman institutions in England.

The people who came to settle in England at the end of the Roman period came from Holland, North Germany, and Denmark. The Venerable Bede, an Anglo-Saxon monk of the joint monastery of Monkwearmouth and Jarrow, writing nearly two hundred years after the event, in about 730, said, "They came from three very powerful nations of Germany, namely the Saxons, Angles, and Jutes. From the Jutes are descended the people of Kent and the Isle of Wight and also those in the province of the West Saxons, who are to this day called the Jutes, situated opposite the Isle of Wight. From the Saxons are descended the East Saxons, the South Saxons, and the West Saxons. From the Angles are descended the East Angles, the Middle Angles, the Mercians, and all the race of the Northumbrians." For convenience these various peoples are known as the Anglo-Saxons or, more simply, the Saxons. The Anglo-Saxons started to call themselves Engle and it is from this word that the name "English" is derived; the term England was not however used until the eleventh century. The Saxon name survives in the names of the counties of Essex and Sussex, while the Eastern counties of Norfolk, Suffolk, and Cambridgeshire are still referred to by their ancient name—East Anglia.

The first Anglo-Saxons came to England before the end of

the Roman period as professional soldiers who helped to defend the country against threatening invaders from Holland, Ireland, and Scotland. They garrisoned the forts of the Saxon shore, which are spread along the Eastern coast of England from Hampshire to Norfolk, and presumably helped to fortify the new fortresses (like that at Caernarvon) on the Welsh coast. They presumably settled down with their families in the rich countryside of Roman Britain and, when the Romans withdrew from Britain they refused to be interested in the defence of the foreign country in which they had settled and probably welcomed the incursions of their cousins from across the North Sea who, as a result of the general land hunger of the period, wanted to find a place in which they could settle in peace. The Anglo-Saxons came in small bands—perhaps such a band was that led by Hengest to the Isle of Thanet in 449—but gradually these bands built themselves up into a mighty military force which was ultimately to conquer Britain.

Dimly across the centuries we hear faint echoes of the resistance that met the Saxons. From the conflicting accounts of coloured legend and dry history we know of a leader named Arthur who, in the last half of the fifth century, fought twelve battles against the Anglo-Saxons and won all of them. He seems to have organized a highly mobile army of Romanized Britons, which went to the aid of the petty kings and chieftains who were struggling against the overwhelming forces of the Anglo-Saxons. The Anglo-Saxon conquest of England was not finally completed, however, until Egbert, King of Wessex, won the last battle against the Britons in 815.

The conquered Britons gradually became submerged in the Saxon population, or else fled to those parts of the British Isles—Scotland, Wales, and Ireland—where the Britons were strong enough to retain political power. It was in these outlying countries that Christianity, introduced into the British Isles by the Romans, survived. Little else remained to remind the Briton or the Saxon of the once powerful Roman Empire. In England many of the great Roman buildings fell into decay; their meaning was lost and they became mysteries, referred to with awe as the works of giants.

Not all the buildings fell into disuse. Many of the towns survived, although not in the splendour of their Roman heyday.

103 Anglo-Saxon Costume

London is described by Bede as "the metropolis of the East Saxons . . . , a market place of many people coming by land and sea". But the elaborate machinery of Roman town government was lost and the towns were only inhabited by a few merchants and craftsmen. Some towns, Silchester and Wroxeter, for example, disappeared completely, but the Roman fountains were still playing at Carlisle when St. Cuthbert visited it, towards the end of the seventh century. The Kentish kings at the end of the sixth century had established their court within the ruins of the Roman city of Canterbury, where some hundred years previously a few Saxon families had built some rather squalid huts in an open space not far from the great Roman theatre. With the coming of Christianity the missionaries used the ancient cities as the centres of their bishoprics, ultimately establishing their cathedrals there. Later on some of the larger cities, like St. Albans, became the seats of large monasteries and the monks used the tumbledown Roman buildings as a quarry for building their churches and living quarters. The walls of many of the Roman cities stood until the Middle Ages when, as at Chester, Lincoln, and Colchester, the Roman walls were incorporated into the city walls. The Roman villa system, however, disappeared completely and the continental invaders laid the foundations of many of the English villages which exist today.

What caused the Anglo-Saxon invasions? Like so many invasions of history and prehistory the roots are hidden deep.

The Anglo-Saxons came to England as a result of disturbance in Central Asia. The Huns came from there, and attacked their neighbours, the Goths, who moved across the Danube, and the Rhine, into the Roman Empire. The Goths captured Rome, and sacked it in 410, and the movement was not stopped until Attila, the King of the Huns, was defeated at Châlons in 451. Another Teutonic people, the Franks, moved into France for the same reason and reached the Loire by 489.

"Westward Ho!" is a very old cry, but in the days of which we are writing it was one fraught with awful peril for civilization. The Roman Empire spelled civilization, and it was a wonderful fabric. The Empire was bounded by the Danube and the Rhine, and across these rivers surged hordes of pagan barbarians, as in older days still the Achaeans had borne down on the Mycenaeans in Greece.

Very truly the historians talk of the Dark Ages; yet through the Darkness come flashes. If we know little of the period, yet what is known is always coloured by life and movement. On one page we shall have to write of Vikings, of bloodshed and battles under the standard of the Raven; on another, of the saving of souls by men like Columba, Augustine, Paulinus, and Aidan. Here in England Christianity had become the great central fact of man's existence, and it was assailed by Odin, and Thor the god of Thunder. It will be part of our tale to show how the Christian Church saved Western civilization. It was a long fight, and before the battle was won Christianity was assailed from another quarter.

Mohammed was born about 570, and his followers conquered Egypt and Palestine 634–40, and Persia in 651. By 709 they had taken North Africa from the Byzantine Empire, and Spain in 711 from the Visigoths. Their further inroads were not stopped until they were defeated by Charles Martel near Poitiers in 732. This was only the beginning of the long struggle between the Cross and Crescent, which was to culminate later in the Crusades. Enough has been written to show that when the Anglo-Saxons came to England, they were not moved to do so because they felt in need of a holiday, but were forced to it by the stress of circumstance. One point should be noted. In their early migrations they had come into contact with Gothic culture in South Russia, and their love of colour and jewellery can probably be traced back to this source.

The Anglo-Saxon Chronicle, compiled in the time of Alfred, 891–2, should be consulted for the details of the invasion. As we do not wish to stain these pages too deeply in blood, we shall content ourselves with one quotation from Bede, to show how desperate the struggle was.

Public as well as private structures were overturned; the priests were everywhere slain before the altars; the prelates and the people, without any respect of persons, were destroyed with fire and sword; nor was there any to bury those who had been thus cruelly slaughtered. Some of the miserable remainder being taken in the mountains, were butchered in heaps. Others, spent with hunger, came forth and submitted themselves to the enemy for food, being destined to undergo perpetual servitude, if they were not killed on the spot.

126

This passage gives a far better idea than any words of ours of what the impact of barbarism meant to the Romano-British civilization, and we are apt to forget the debt we may owe to the Britons today, in keeping Christianity alive in the West. In fact, we may not even think of them as Christians, until we remember that St. Alban was martyred as early as 304, here in England. St. Patrick went to Ireland about 432 and it was the Irish Church which sent Columba to Iona about 563, and from Iona, Aidan went at a later date to Holy Isle, as we shall presently see. We must always remember that Great Britain was an outlier on the Roman Empire; a North-West Province which was the outpost of its civilization, and by its island position cut off from Rome by the barbarian inroads. It may well be that the whole history of this country would have been different, if the Irish Church had not humanized life in the West, while the Anglo-Saxons were giving a very fair imitation of the Devil and all his works elsewhere.

Before we trace the work of the Church in more detail, it may be well to go back and endeavour to find out if our Anglo-Saxon ancestors had any other qualities wherewith to qualify their ferocity.

Tacitus, who knew the breed, wrote: "They live apart, each by himself, as woodside, plain, or fresh spring attracts him" and this has remained a characteristic of Englishmen ever since; they have little civic pride, but love the country. Tacitus of course did not mean solitary men living by themselves, or even single families, as today, in modest little houses in the suburbs. Even as late as the time of Sir Thomas More, we read that he built himself a house at Chelsea, where he lived with his wife, his son, and his daughter-in-law, his three daughters, and their husbands, with eleven grandchildren. In Anglo-Saxon times the families which lived together were even larger than this, and more like a tribe or clan. Bede always counts, not the number of inhabitants in a province, but tells you how many families it contained. He also throws an interesting sidelight on family customs. He wrote of one "Orric, surnamed Oisc, from whom the kings of Kent are wont to be called Oiscings", and again "The son of Tytilus whose father was Uuffa, from whom the kings of the East Angles are called Uuffings." If we turn again

127

to Bede we find that the kings at first were what we should call chiefs, "for those Ancient Saxons have no king, but several lords that rule their nation; and when any war happens, they cast lots indifferently, and on whomsoever the lot falls, him they follow and obey during the war; but as soon as the war is ended, all those lords are again equal in power". When the Saxons came to England, we must think of these chiefs settling down, and calling their home Uuffingham, because it was the home of the Uuffings, who were the descendants of Uuffa.

From such simple beginnings our English villages have grown up. The chief built his Hall, and grouped around it were the huts of his followers, and the bowers for the women-folk. The village had a meeting-place, or moot, where important decisions were taken; it also had a well or a spring for water. The whole was girt round with a ditch and bank, with a palisaded fence on top. There were the common fields, and outside all the mark, where the stranger coming must blow his horn or risk death. The freeman was the freeholder of part of the land, and there cannot have been many slaves in the bands of warriors who came first, but later the Britons who were captured were enslaved, and as society became more settled, and the chieftains became kings, some men went up, and others sank into a servile class.

Domesday Book, completed in 1086, mentions parishes of the time of Edward the Confessor which still remain, and which had their beginnings in the time we write of. The hall of the chief became the hall of the lord, and his chapel, built when he became a Christian, developed into the parish church. Bede writes of an inn, and there would have been a mill for grinding corn—a water mill, for instance, has recently been discovered and excavated at Old Windsor, Berkshire.

This is the outline on to which we have to graft fuller details, and our first step will be to familiarize ourselves with the appearance of the Anglo-Saxons, so that we may be able to fit them into the picture.

We may take it that the dress of the first Saxons who arrived here resembled that illustrated in fig. *140, Prehistoric Times*; this again was like that of the barbarians shown on the Trajan

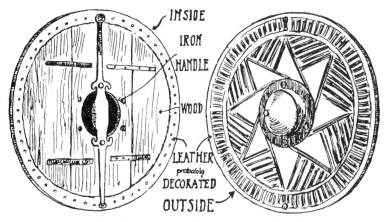

INSIDE
IRON
HANDLE
WOOD
LEATHER
probably
DECORATED
OUTSIDE

104   A reconstructed Anglo-Saxon shield

Column, and must have been common to the tribes outside the Empire, across the Rhine and Danube. The Anglo-Saxon dress was a development of this.

In fig. *103*, the first figure on the left is a Thane. He wore a shirt, and breeches, sometimes to the ankles, and at others cut off at the knee, when hose like leggings were added, and fastened by cross garters which were part of the leather shoes. These latter were sometimes gilded. The breeches were probably fastened at the waist, by a belt passed through loops. Over the shirt, a wool, or linen, tunic reaching to the knee was worn. This was belted at the waist, and had long sleeves tight at the wrist, and fastened with metal clasps. The cloak was fastened on breast or shoulder with a brooch. For everyday use caps of Phrygian shape were worn.

The next man has much the same clothes, but is shown bearing arms. He carries arms which would indicate that he is a chieftain of some importance. His tunic is a coat of mail formed of iron rings sewn on to the strong cloth. His helmet has an iron frame, filled in between with horn with a boar on the crest (see Beowulf, page 136). The spear was the commonest weapon in the early pagan days; sometimes it had wings on it(*105*) and the socket was formed by hammering the iron round until the sides met. The shaft of ash, 6 to 7 feet long, had an iron ferrule. Some were thrown as javelins. The early swords were formidable

129

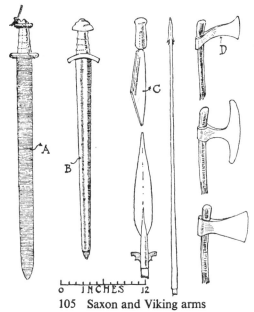

105 Saxon and Viking arms

weapons, a yard long, with a wooden scabbard (*105*, A). The later types had a tapered blade, as B; Scramas-axes were sword-like knives, as C.

Battle-axes were used, and some were thrown (*105*, D). Shields were of wood, sometimes covered with hide, painted or set with semi-precious stones or gilt-bronze mounts, sometimes oval, and at others round. They measured between 1 foot 6 inches and 3 feet in diameter. Fig. *104* shows the hand-grip of one. The bow was not very much used.

The central figure in fig. *103* shows how women were dressed. They had one linen undergarment, and a tunic to the feet. Sometimes there were two tunics girdled at the waist, the inner having long sleeves, and the outer shorter and wider ones. Over these came the mantle, hanging down at back and front, in a way which suggests a poncho pattern with central hole for the head. The brooches, which we discuss later, appear to have been worn in pairs. The head was covered with a silk or linen wrap. The women wore girdles (girdle hangers like chatelaines have been found in their graves), and they had little bags.

They adorned themselves with fine barbaric necklaces; big lumps of amber, crystal, amethyst, or beads of glass coloured in many ways. One in the British Museum has barrel-shaped gold beads which alternate with gold-mounted garnet pendants. Sometimes these were worn festooned across the chest, or as bracelets.

We cannot illustrate all the beautiful things which were used. Belts had jewelled buckles, and there were armlets, and rings.

Pins of all patterns were made; Ireland was the home of what are called hand-pins, with the head cranked like a modern tie-pin. The horse was trapped out as beautifully as his master. Children's dress was a miniature edition of that of their parents.

The ceorl on the right of fig. *103* would have worn the same type of clothes as his master, but everything would have been simpler and rougher. He carried no sword. This was the weapon of the earl or thane.

This will be a good place in which to show the development of the brooches which were used to fasten the cloaks. These can

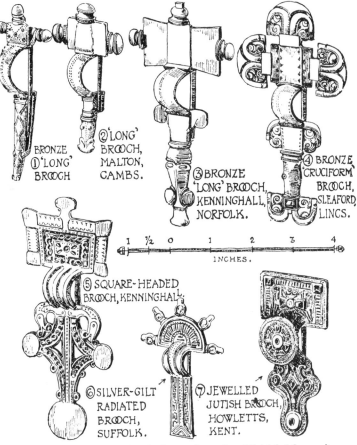

106 Early (Pagan) Anglo-Saxon brooches (*British Museum*)

be traced back to South Russia, where they were used by the Goths. Fig. *106* has been drawn to show some of the developments of the main types of brooch. 1, probably East Anglian, is perhaps as early as the fifth century, and the same pattern, with the horse-like head on the foot, is found as well in Scandinavia. All these brooches are glorified versions of our old friend the safety-pin, but with a spring on both sides of the head (see *Prehistoric Times*, fig. *150*, 5 which shows the beginnings in the Bronze and Early Iron Ages).

Fig. *106*, 2, shows the next development. The knobs on the bar are now cast in one piece with the brooch. This type dates from the end of the fifth century. 3 shows a further and later development. 4 illustrates why this type is called "cruciform"; it dates from the seventh century, and is a beautiful piece, with small silver panels on the arms of the cross, and garnet inlay on the nostrils of the horse. 5 is a square-headed brooch which resembles types started in Denmark; this is earlier than 4, dating from about 500. 6 is a radiated brooch, of which parallels have been found in the Crimea; this is a fifth-century type. 7 has its own peculiar Jutish design.

The Anglo-Saxons used as well circular brooches. Sometimes they were plain and sometimes saucer-shaped with a cast design in the centre. Occasionally they were made of an embossed plate cemented on to a disc with vertical edge, the pin at the back being hinged.

The jewelled circular brooches found in Kent are extraordinarily fine. Some are like the disc applied to the bow of 7. This is called the keystone brooch, because the garnet inlays are mounted in the form of wedges, like the keystones of an arch, the central boss being of ivory, or some similar white substance. Others are far more elaborately decorated with garnets and blue glass to imitate lapis lazuli, and gold filigree work applied to the background. The Kentish jewellery has parallels in the Rhineland and Italy, and its best period is about the year 600.

There are quoit brooches, so called because of their shape, made of silver, partly gilt. There were wonderful developments of the Early Iron Age penannular types, shaped like an incomplete ring; some tenth-century brooches had pins as much as two feet long.

Fine jewellery needs good material to show it off, and there is evidence that the Anglo-Saxon women were expert weavers. When William the Conqueror returned from England to France for the first time, his Norman subjects were astonished by the garments he had obtained in England—they were much finer than any that had ever been seen in France. Gold threads have been found in graves, generally in a position which suggests that they were originally woven into a head-dress. This may have been produced in the same way as the ephod made for Aaron, "they did beat the gold into thin plates, and cut it into wires, to work it in the blue, and in the purple, and in the scarlet, and in the fine linen, with cunning work".

This joyous use of colour was not confined to costume, but was common to everything. King Alfred, for example, made his grandson Athelstan "a knight unusually early, giving him a scarlet coat, a belt studded with diamonds and a Saxon sword with a golden scabbard". He must have presented a very colourful appearance.

The materials of which we have been writing were of course woven on a loom, and drawings in the manuscripts suggest that this had been developed. As we last saw it (in *Prehistoric Times*, fig. *114*) the warp was stretched by warp weights; now a bottom roller was added, which got rid of the weights, and enabled a greater length of material to be made. Blunt iron blades, like short two-edged swords, have been found in women's graves, and these are thought to have been used to pack the weft threads together on to those of the warp. The weaving was done as described in *Prehistoric Times*, page 158.

An interesting object is the work-box (*107*) which was found in a grave, and is now in the British Museum. It is of gilt-bronze and contained thread, wool, linen, and needles.

Here we may give a note on ecclesiastical costumes. In the priest's vestments the long white tunic became the alb. The upper tunic with looser and shorter sleeves, the dalmatic. The mantle developed into the chasuble, and its hood became the cope. The more important vestments were richly embroidered with gold and coloured thread.

There is also the traditional costume in which Our Lord and the Saints and Angels are always shown. First comes a long

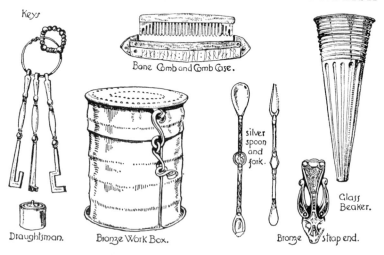

Keys

Bone Comb and Comb Case.

silver spoon and fork.

Glass Beaker.

Draughtsman.   Bronze Work Box.   Bronze Strap end.

107   Anglo-Saxon workmanship

sleeved tunic, then there is a mantle, one end of which hangs down from the left shoulder in front, the remainder being taken behind the back, and passed under the right shoulder and across the front to be draped over the left arm or shoulder. This dress is much in the classical fashion of the Roman toga described on page 53.

Having obtained some idea of the appearance of the Saxons, we must search for the local colour of their background, and we cannot do better than study Bede's History. Its date, about 730, makes it very important. The final conquest of the Britons, in 815, was approaching; the Danes had not yet appeared to plunder and destroy, so the picture given by Bede is of the apex of Anglo-Saxon civilization.

He opens with a description,

Britain, an island in the ocean, formerly called Albion . . . excels for grain and trees, and is well adapted for feeding cattle and beasts of burden. It also produces vines in some places, and has plenty of land and water-fowls of several sorts; it is remarkable also for rivers abounding in fish, and plentiful springs. It has the greatest plenty of salmon and eels; seals are frequently taken, and dolphins, as also whales; besides many sorts of shell-fish, such as mussels, in which are often found excellent pearls of all colours, red, purple, violet, and green, but mostly white. There is also a great abundance of cockles, of which the scarlet dye is made; a most beautiful colour which never fades with the heat of the sun or the washing of the rain; but the older it is the more beautiful it becomes. It has both salt and hot springs, and from them flow rivers which furnish hot baths proper for all ages and sexes, and arranged according.

Bede mentions copper, iron, lead, silver, and jet,

which is black and sparkling, glittering at the fire, and when heated drives away serpents; being warmed with rubbing, it holds fast whatever is applied to it, like amber. (He goes on to say) this island at present, contains five nations, the English, Britons, Scots (meaning the Irish), Picts, and Latins (Romanized Britons), each in its own peculiar dialect cultivating the sublime study of Divine truth. The Latin tongue is, by the study of the Scriptures, become common to all the rest.

Even in Bede's time, the people do not appear to have been town dwellers, because he writes,

The Island was *formerly* embellished with twenty-eight noble cities, besides innumerable castles, which were all strongly secured with walls, towers, gates and locks. [Some of the Roman towns, though, were being used, because we read in 604] The East Saxons, who are divided from Kent by the river Thames, and border on the Eastern sea. Their metropolis is the city of London, which is situated on the bank of the aforesaid river, and is the mart of many nations resorting to it by sea and land.

We do not know how far the Roman Londinium had been destroyed, but there must have been considerable remains to influence the Saxon builders. Perhaps they patched them up here and there, and added timber buildings when new ones were necessary. Benedict Biscop, who built the monastery at Jarrow, where Bede lived, is said to have been "the first person who introduced in England constructors of stone edifices, as well as the makers of glass windows", meaning of course the first after the Romans.

In 710, the king of the Picts wrote to Abbot Ceolfrid, of Jarrow, to send him architects "to build a church in his nation after the Roman manner". Mellitus, bishop of the East Saxons, built the church of St. Paul in the city of London, and this may have been in the Roman manner. We discuss this again in King Alfred's time.

We will now consider the hall of the Chief. This was to remain, until the days of Elizabeth, as the central feature of the house in which all the household met for meals and jollity. Even today, the big house in a village is very often called the Hall. The bowers, and kitchens, which at first were separate buildings, were gradually tacked on the body of the hall, until in the fourteenth and fifteenth centuries they all come under the same roof, and the modern house takes shape.

If we turn to Beowulf, the great Anglo-Saxon poem, we find the early type of hall described, and there are many interesting details of everyday life.

The only manuscript of Beowulf is in the British Museum. This dates from about 1000, but deals with life in the first half of the sixth century. The poem opens with an account of the passing of Scyld, the Warrior King, who lived in earlier days and gave the Danes their name of Scyldings. Scyld was carried down to his ship, and placed by the mast, the dead eyes looking ahead. Weapons and treasure were put aboard and, with his standard high above his head, the ship was pushed out on the flood, to sail into the unknown seas beyond the horizon. Then we read of Beowulf, who was a prince of the Geats, of the Baltic island of Gotland. He went to Denmark to visit Hrothgar, who had built a Mead Hall, named Heorot, as a habitation for his retainers. This hall was a lofty and gabled building of wood, and gold-bespangled, and the door was strengthened by forged bands. A pathed way led up to it.These were not sufficient to keep out the fiend Grendel, who came at night and carried off the warriors sleeping after the banquet. Men sought beds among the outbuildings to escape.

Then came Beowulf in his fresh tarred ship, over the sea. With him were fourteen champions, above whose cheek-guards shone the boar-images covered with gold. Their corslets were hard, hand-locked, and glistened, each gleaming ring of iron chinked in their harness. Landing in Denmark, they went to Heorot. Here they put their shields against the wall, and sat on the benches.

Hrothgar was not in the hall. He had a chamber close by where he sat with his nobles. Beowulf went there, by a path between, and explained his mission, and was after entertained at a banquet in the hall. Wealhtheow, the queen, entered and bore the mead cup to Beowulf. He and his men slept in the hall, and there came Grendel, and killed one man. The monster was attacked by Beowulf, but escaped, with the loss of an arm, only to die later in the mere where he lived.

Again there was a banquet, and the hall was decorated with gold embroidered tapestries. The song was sung, the gleeman's lay. Then mirth rose high, the noise of revelry was clearly heard; cup-bearers proferred wine from curious vessels. The men then slept in the hall.

> They cleared the bench-boards, it was spread about with beds and bolsters. They set war-bucklers at their heads, the shining shield-wood. There on the bench, above each noble, was exposed the helmet, prominent in war, the ringed mail-coat, the proud spear-shaft. It was ever their practice to be ready for the fray at home or in the field.

But Grendel's mother came to avenge his death, and carried off a noble. Beowulf was not in the hall, having had a separate lodging assigned to him as a special honour. He went to the King's bower, and then led a band on horseback, who traced the steps of the monster to the mere. Here Beowulf put on his armour and went down into the lake, and swimming to the bottom, found there a cavern where no water harmed him in any way. Here was fought the fight with the she-wolf of the deep. His own sword failed him, but in the cavern he found an old titanic sword, and with it gained the victory, and having killed the mother, cut the head off the dead body of Grendel.

The watchers on the bank viewed the blood-stained waters with gloomy foreboding, and the disheartened Danes went home. Later Beowulf swam up with Grendel's head and found his own men waiting. They returned to Heorot, where once again there was great rejoicing, and Hrothgar made a fine speech congratulating Beowulf, but warned him that though God deals out to mankind many gifts, the soul's guardian may sleep, and man wax insolent and arrogant, and so be "struck at the heart under his armour, by the piercing arrow—the crooked strange behests of the malignant spirit".

Beowulf returned to the land of the Geats, and told his king, Hygelac, of his adventures, seated opposite to him in the hall. Later he became king himself, and ruled well until his own land was oppressed by a dragon, 50 feet long, winged, and vomiting fire. The monster lived in a barrow, "the primeval earth-dwelling contained within it rocky arches", and guarded there a hoard of treasure. A drinking bowl was stolen by a thrall, and the dragon ravaged the countryside in revenge. Then Beowulf, now an old man, girded on his armour for his last fight and, killing the dragon, was himself killed by it.

His funeral pyre was made on the cliff by the sea, and around it were hung helmets, shields, and corslets, and then Beowulf was laid in its midst. When his body was consumed by fire, they heaped up a barrow on the remains, and in it placed the treasure of the dragon, "where it still exists, as unprofitable to men as it had been before".

The poem is of extraordinary interest, because it gives the outlook on life of the ordinary man. With Bede we see the world through a monk's eyes, but in Beowulf we have the thoughts of the warrior. It must have been sung by poets in a thousand halls until some Saxon Homer set it out in proper form.

There are many details in the poem which suggest the hall of Heorot was a timber-framed building, rather like a glorified barn. We have attempted a reconstruction of the exterior in fig. *108*, and of the interior on the jacket.

One important detail of these early halls should be noted: the principal seat instead of being on a raised dais at the end, as it was in the later mediaeval halls, was placed in the centre of the north side. The chief guest had his seat opposite on the south side, and here was a window. Women sat on cross benches at the end. The fire was placed centrally.

Bede recounts how a traveller came to a village and entered a house where the neighbours were feasting. "They sat long at supper and drank hard, with a great fire in the middle of the room; it happened that the sparks flew up and caught the top of the house, which being made of wattles and thatch, was presently in a flame."

108   An imaginary reconstruction of an Anglo-Saxon homestead

We see in Beowulf how there were sleeping-rooms in other buildings. In one saga we find that these were on the first floor, reached by an outer staircase, because a guest, going up to bed, opened the wrong door and fell into the mead vat under instead.

At Yeavering, Northumberland, traces of a hall similar to Heorot have been uncovered, by careful excavation, within the last few years. Traces of four halls of different periods were found, each nearly a hundred feet long. Two had porches at either end while the other two were rectangular in plan, but elaborately buttressed. Yeavering was a royal site and as a consequence there were a number of small halls surrounding the main hall. Most of these must be considered as the private halls of noble retainers; one was a servants' dormitory and one a pagan temple which was later put to Christian use. Unfortunately only the ground-plan of the houses survives, so it is practically impossible to reconstruct the upper works.

We know remarkably little about the physical construction of the Anglo-Saxon house used by the peasant and small farmer. Only the richer houses are described in the literature and, with the exception of a few weaving sheds at Sutton Courtenay, Berkshire, and a few rather shapeless wooden houses excavated at Bourton-on-the-Water, Gloucestershire, English archaeologists have not yet uncovered the remains of the houses of the farmer and the peasant. The English archaeologist must look to Germany and Scandinavia where a great deal of excavation and research has enabled us to build up a general picture of the poorer house of the period. It seems reasonable to assume that the Anglo-Saxons built houses in the manner of their Germanic forebears, houses of the type described by Tacitus.

Tacitus, writing in the first century A.D., said that

> none of the Germanic peoples dwell in cities, and they do not even tolerate houses which are built in rows. They dwell apart, and at a distance from one another, according to the preference which they may have for the stream, the plain, or the grove. . . . They do not make use of stone cut from the quarry, or of tiles; for every kind of building they make use of unshapely wood, which falls short of beauty or attractiveness. They carefully colour some parts of their buildings with earth which is so clear and bright as to resemble painting and coloured designs.

At Warendorf, in Westphalia, German archaeologists have excavated some eighty buildings of an Anglo-Saxon village. Many of these were small outhouses, working sheds, barns, and cow sheds. Reconstructions of the various types of building found at Warendorf are illustrated in fig. *109*. The long house with the steeply-pitched roof at the top of the picture is typical of the dwelling houses that were found on the site. The ground plans and the remains of the walls of about six of these houses were found and from this it was possible to reconstruct the whole building. These long houses varied in length between 42 and 87 feet and were the most important type of building found on the site. We must presume that the Anglo-Saxon farmer lived in such a building with his family. The serfs and servants apparently lived in smaller houses of the types shown in fig. *109*, 2, 3, and 5. But many outhouses were used to sleep in and we can imagine the weaving women sleeping in the weaving shed that was excavated by Mr. Leeds at Sutton Courtenay, Berkshire, which, like house No. 5 in fig. *109*, was partly sunk into the ground.

The houses, as Tacitus wrote, were constructed of wood. Over a frame like that illustrated in fig. *110* were laid either overlapping planks or wattle hurdles covered with mud daub,

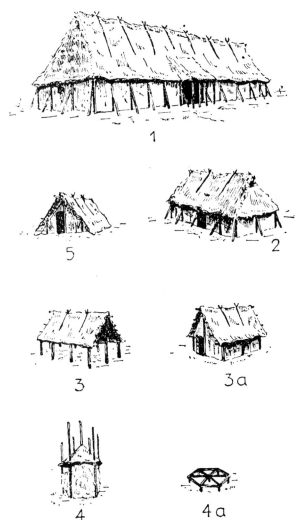

109 Reconstructions of different types of Saxon
buildings at Warendorf, Germany

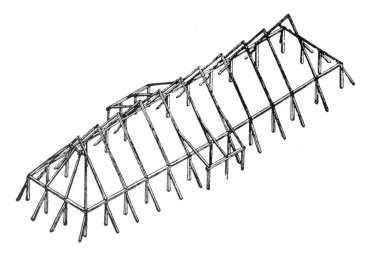

110   Reconstruction of frame-work of a house from Warendorf

which may have been, as Tacitus says, coloured. The roofs were presumably covered with thatch, although there is some evidence that in the larger houses wooden shingles were used.

There were many varieties of house in the Anglo-Saxon period, some had stone foundations, and some may even have had stone walls, but in general outward appearance most of them would look rather like the houses from Warendorf

111   Construction of wall and roof of timber-framed house

142

illustrated in fig. *109.*
In some of the houses
both the animals and
the humans would
live side by side,
separated only by
a low wall or a
thin wooden or
wattle screen. The
fire would be in the
centre of the floor
and there was prob-
ably a hole in the

112 Urn with implements found in it
(*British Museum*)

roof to allow the smoke to escape, but in the depths of a cold
winter, or when it rained, the hole would be closed and the
smoke would be left to find its own way out through the various
chinks and cracks that must have abounded in these roughly
built houses. The cooking was done over this fire and the food
was served to the members of the household who would eat
it sitting on the floor or on benches running
along the sides of the house. In the poorer
houses the whole family would sleep in the
same room, warmed by the dying embers
of the central fire.

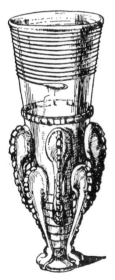

Having dealt with the house, and how
it was built, we will discuss the table furniture of the Anglo-Saxons. The jacket
illustration shows a banquet in progress.
Each man carried his own knife. Fig. *112*
shows one of these, from a burial, where it
had been placed for the use of its owner in
the spirit world. Spoons and forks were
extremely rare and would only be owned
by the rich, and even the rich would use
only a knife at table.

The table glass was very beautiful; not a
clear white, but in ambers, blues, and greens,
decorated in a very glass-blowing way with
tears, or gouts(*113*) of the molten glass,

113 Anglo-
Saxon glass
(*British Museum*)

143

114 Anglo-Saxon glass (*British Museum*)

which being hollow, are in some miraculous way connected with the inside so that the wine could flow into them. Others have spidery threads laid on. Often they had no foot to stand on, and the contents had to be tossed off at a draught. Fig. *107* shows one of these. Other patterns are shown in figs. *113* and *114*.

Pottery of course was made, and figs. *112* and *117* show cinerary urns. Fig. *116* shows a rare jug from the British Museum, dating from the fifth century. Its handle is perforated as a spout. Fig. *115* shows a bottle of reddish ware. This is Jutish, and the Jutes' pottery, like their jewellery, was different from that of the Angles and Saxons. In the early part of the Anglo-Saxon period the pottery was hand-made, and it was not until the eighth century that wheel-turned pottery was re-introduced into England. There is one exception to this rule; in Kentish Anglo-Saxon graves a reddish wheel-turned pottery is found. But this may have been imported from the Low Countries.

The houses were lighted by candles, rush lights, or oil-burning lamps. William of Malmesbury tells how when Ethelred II was a boy of 10 years old,

115 Jutish bottle (*British Museum*)

144

he so irritated his furious mother by his weeping, that not having a whip at hand, she beat the little innocent with some candles she had snatched up . . . on this account he dreaded candles during the rest of his life.

116 Anglo-Saxon jug
(*British Museum*)

When we turn to the personal belongings of the Anglo-Saxons, we shall have to study these in connection with their burials. This may sound a little dismal, but all the everyday things we possess of the period have been found in graves. With one exception (at Sutton Courtenay, which is not very helpful), there is no site which can be instanced as Anglo-Saxon, in the way that Silchester can be of Roman Britain.

Graves, however, are a wonderful indication of the outlook of a people. The heathen sometimes burned his dead, and buried arms and implements with the ashes, for use in the spirit world. In doing this, he was more helpful to the archaeologist than the Christian, who was buried, to await the Resurrection, without any such aids.

From the Old Stone Age we have traced how the changes were rung through the centuries, between burial by burning—cremation—and by interring the unburned body in the earth, called inhumation. At the end of the Roman period inhumation became general. This was altered once more, because some Saxons burned their dead. Fig. *117* shows one of the cinerary urns from the British Museum. These are grey, brown, or black and, what is very extraordinary, they are not turned on a wheel

117 A Pagan burial urn
(*British Museum*)

145

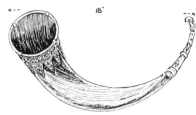

118   A drinking-horn
(*British Museum*)

but are hand-made, like the prehistoric pottery described in *Prehistoric Times*. Cremation seems to have appealed very especially to the Anglians, and was retained longer by them than by the Saxons. The Jutes always favoured inhumation.

Fig. *112* shows a cinerary urn from the British Museum, with the implements which were buried with the ashes. Smaller pots perhaps contained food and drink for use on the journey to the other world. In the British Museum can be seen the contents of a grave of a chieftain at Taplow. This was dug 12 feet long, by 8 feet wide, by 6 feet deep, and east to west, but the head was at the east, instead of at the west, as in Christian usage. The spear lay inverted at the side of the skeleton and the sword was placed ready to hand. The gold buckle, and clasps of the belt, are very beautiful, set with garnets and lapis lazuli. Above the head were two shields, an iron knife and ring. To the south-east were a bucket and bronze bowl. There were glass cups, and the remains of a large tub which had been placed over the thighs of the warrior. Two drinking horns(*118*) were there to quench his thirst, and thirty bone draughtsmen accompanied him to while away the time. There is another set at the British Museum made from horses' teeth.

The grave at Taplow was covered with a barrow or mound of earth, and its furniture gives us a very good idea of the belongings of a chieftain. Heathen burials ceased with the final conversion of the English by Wilfrid about 681. Tombstones were used in later Saxon times.

In the summer of 1939 there was dug from British soil one of the richest treasures it can ever have contained. This was the celebrated Sutton Hoo treasure, the greatest single find known to British archaeology.

A Saxon sea-going ship, eighty foot long, was found beneath a barrow on a sandy heath near the Suffolk coast. The barrow was one of a small compact group of barrows situated on the bank of the River Deben, opposite the town of Woodbridge, about ten miles from Ipswich. Three or four hundred years ago grave-robbers had attempted to plunder the barrow, and the hole they dug into it from the top was still visible. The robbers had missed the centre of the ship, where the marvellous treasure lay, by a matter of inches.

The professional archaeologists who excavated the barrow in 1939 used very different methods from those of the fly-by-night bunglers who had sought mere loot. Their work ranks among the most careful and systematic excavations ever undertaken. It seems almost incredible, but the little band of scholars went about their work with such patient thoroughness that they laid bare the entire outline of the ancient Saxon vessel, despite the fact that its timbers had long since rotted completely away. All they had to guide them were the iron clench-nails which once held the planks together, and a dark stain in the sand where the wood had been. With these meagre clues they reconstructed the original appearance of the once proud ship, an early relative of the Gokstad ship (140). Unlike the Gokstad ship and other Viking ships, the Sutton Hoo ship does not appear to have had a sail. Instead, it was rowed along by a crew of thirty-eight oarsmen.

In the centre of the ship the Saxon burial-party had erected a wooden cabin. They then strewed bracken over it, and heaped above it an oval mound of earth faced with turf. In the cabin were deposited the personal effects of the powerful chieftain in whose honour the ship had been dragged from the estuary to its resting-place on the upland heath. There was the chieftain's iron standard, over six foot high and topped with the emblem of a stag. There was a huge ceremonial whetstone, near which lay the great sword it may once have sharpened. The blade was rusted for ever in its leather scabbard, but the hilt still gleamed with gold and rich jewels. There were the remains of the big shield the warrior bore on his left arm, and also the crushed remnants of his fine helmet, ornamented with bronze and silver plaques and provided with projecting pieces to protect his ears and neck. To the front of the helmet was fixed a fearsome-looking mask, a hinged vizor worked in silver, bronze, and garnet, to shield the wearer's face. Near by were the chieftain's throwing-axe, and his hawberk, or coat of mail.

There were other objects in profusion: iron spears, cauldrons

119   Designs on the silver mounts of drinking-horns dug from a barrow at
Sutton Hoo, Suffolk, in 1939 (*British Museum*)

and buckets, bronze bowls, and silver drinking-horns. Beneath
a great silver dish, bearing the imperial stamp of Anastasius I
of Byzantium, was a fluted silver bowl with the head of a classical
goddess in the centre. Near a set of nine shallow silver bowls
lay two silver spoons, each ten inches in length, with the names
"Paulos" and "Saulos" engraved on them in Greek characters,
symbols no doubt of some ancient christening ceremony.

Even these splendid trophies do not exhaust the total of the
discoveries made at Sutton Hoo. For the most magnificent
pieces of all are unquestionably the jewels, scattered in profusion
among the effects of the dead leader. Figs. *121–3* illustrate
some of the choicest of them, but there are many more. They
were given by their owner, Mrs. Pretty, to the British Museum,
where they are now displayed. All the gold pieces except the
great belt-buckle(*121*) are jewelled with garnets, a beautiful deep
red semi-precious stone, and there are over four thousand tiny
pieces of garnet in the whole collection of jewellery, each one
cut individually to fit snugly into its little golden pit. From among
the many buckles and clasps and mounts and buttons we may
single out the purse-lid(*123*), enriched with plaques once set
in a base of ivory or bone. The purse contained thirty-seven
gold coins, and its catch and hinges, like those of all the other
jewellery, still work perfectly after thirteen centuries at the

120 Trajan's Column: Dacians in flight, native dwellings being fired, and captive heads exposed on poles in background

121, 122 The great gold belt-buckle and (*right*) a hinged gold clasp decorated with garnets, mosaic glass and filigree. Dug from a Barrow at Sutton Hoo, Suffolk in 1939 (*British Museum*)

123 Purse-lid, with gold frame, fittings, and ornamental plaques, decorated with garnets and mosaic glass. Dug from a Barrow at Sutton Hoo, Suffolk in 1939 (*British Museum*)

bottom of the earthen barrow. The intricate patterns on the objects from Sutton Hoo, so savage yet so sophisticated, merit a special study. The weird birds and animals and reptiles are twisted and contorted into a hundred subtle shapes. It must be apparent to everyone who sees these specimens of their handiwork that the Saxon craftsmen were not only gifted metalworkers but superb artists as well.

The Sutton Hoo barrow is not a burial but a cenotaph, a monument to a soldier who died fighting and whose remains were not recovered by his followers, for no body was found in the barrow. The notion that the grave is a cenotaph happens to agree, as it falls out, with the strongest candidature for the monument. It would seem that we have at Sutton Hoo a token burial of a king of East Anglia called Aethelhere, who was drowned by a flood on the battlefield of Winwaed in Yorkshire. Aethelhere had allied himself with the pagan King Penda of Mercia against Christian Northumbria, and the disastrous fight at Winwaed, described by the Venerable Bede, took place in A.D. 655. At present the authorities incline to the opinion that Aethelhere's court trappings were buried at Sutton Hoo, as a token of respect, by his followers. We thus have at Sutton Hoo a particularly sumptuous example of the lavish funerals accorded to pagan monarchs, one of the last of its kind ever undertaken in Britain.

The practice of medicine in Anglo-Saxon times seems to have consisted of faith healing, assisted by rough surgery. In 660, the physician Cynefrid operated on Queen Etheldrida, who had "a very great swelling under her jaw". "And I was ordered", said he, "to lay open that swelling, to let out the noxious matter in it."

Again in 698, the surgeons were puzzled by a youth whose eyelid had a great swelling on it. They "applied their medicines to ripen it, but in vain. Some said it ought to be cut off; others opposed it, for fear of worse consequences."

Bleeding was a popular cure for many diseases. One young girl who was very ill was bled in the arm. A bishop was asked to help, but said,

> You did very indiscreetly and unskilfully to bleed her in the fourth day of the moon; for I remember that Archbishop Theodore,

151

of blessed memory, said that bleeding at that time was very dangerous, when the light of the moon and the tide of the ocean is increasing; and what can I do to the girl if she is like to die?

Matters were not arranged very cheerfully for the patients. An earl's servant had lost the use of all his limbs, and again a bishop was called in and "saw him in a dying condition, and the coffin at his side".

Bede writes, "a sudden pestilence (664) also depopulated the southern coasts of Britain, and afterwards extending into the province of the Northumbrians, ravaged the country far and near, and destroyed a great multitude of men". These plagues recurred through the centuries, and were caused by lack of knowledge of hygiene and the fouling of the water supply. The jointed drain pipes of Mycenae, and the uses of the sewers of Roman Britain were forgotten.

The Church in Saxon times introduced the practice of burying within the sacred building. Bede wrote of another practice which the doctors of today would hardly recommend. St. Chad was buried and

> the place of the sepulchre is a wooden monument, made like a little house, covered, having a hole in the wall, through which those that go thither for devotion usually put in their hand and take out some of the dust, which they put into water and give to sick cattle or men to drink, upon which they are presently eased of their infirmity, and restored to health.

However, we shall have a totally wrong idea of the Anglo-Saxons, if we think of them as ignorant barbarians. At the end of our first period, in 781, before the Danes had wasted the country, Alcuin, a Northumbrian educated at York, went to the Court of Charlemagne and gave him a thorough knowledge of logic, rhetoric, and astronomy. The man who was governing all Western Europe, with the exception of Spain, turned to England for instruction. This is not surprising when we consider that at this period England was a storehouse of knowledge; York, for example, before it was sacked by the Vikings, had the largest library north of the Alps.

Bede tells us that, as early as 635, King Sigebert

> being desirous to imitate the good institutions which he had seen in France, he set up a school for youth (at Seaham or Dunwich)

152

to be instructed in literature. [Theodore (699) assisted by Hadrian] gathered a crowd of disciples . . . and, together with the books of holy writ, they also taught them the arts of ecclesiastical poetry, astronomy, and arithmetic. A testimony of which is, that there are still living at this day some of their scholars, who are as well versed in the Greek and Latin tongues as in their own.

Children started their schooling at an early age. Bede wrote of a boy, Esica, not above three years old, placed in a monastery to pursue his studies.

We do not hear much about games in Saxon times, perhaps because life was so interesting that it was more amusing to play at being grown up, with romps in between, as the Eskimo children do today. They have small weapons and implements and learn their job by playing at it. Small Saxon battle-axes have been found which suggest this. Here is a note on horse racing.

We came into a plain and open road, well adapted for galloping our horses. The young men that were with him and particularly those of the laity, began to entreat the bishop to give them leave to gallop, and make trial of the goodness of their horses.

Chess was played, as was some form of draughts.

Bede was not only the first of the English historians, but a classical scholar as well. He referred to Plato's "Republic" when he wrote: "a certain worldly writer most truly said, that the world would be most happy if either kings were philosophers, or philosophers were kings".

It was in a monastery at Whitby, that Caedmon, one of the lay brothers, first received inspiration, and became the father of English poetry.

Gildas, who has been called the British Jeremiah, wrote his history as early as 545. It might have been of supreme interest, but, unfortunately for us, the book, starting as a history, very speedily develops into a moral lecture. Gildas has hardly a good word to say for the Britons, who were delivered into the hands of the Saxons because of their sins; then the turn of the Saxons comes, and they are denounced as being "a race hateful both to God and man". Gildas has one interesting reference to the "diabolical idols . . . of which we still see some mouldering

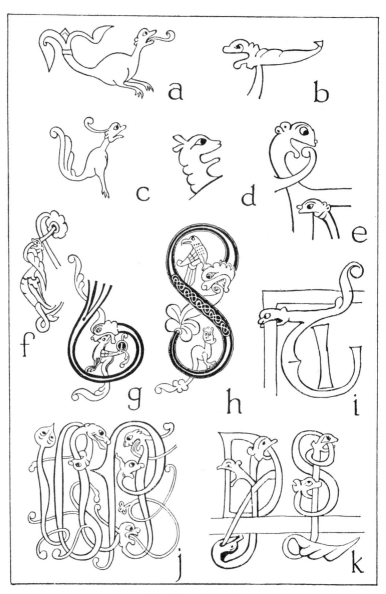

124   Saxon initials

away within or without the deserted temples, with stiff and deformed features as was customary." As he refers also to walled towns, these architectural remains must have been survivals of Romano-British building.

125 Figure from the Book of Kells

Geoffrey of Monmouth lived much later, between 1100–54. He must have been a delightful person. One phrase gives a taste of his quality: "The island was then called Albion and was inhabited by none but a few giants." As we have not yet interested ourselves in the everyday life of giants we have not drawn on Geoffrey for information. He wrote, or, as he himself says, translated into Latin, a very ancient book of British History. He did this because neither Gildas nor Bede said anything "of those kings who lived here before the Incarnation of Christ, nor of Arthur". Bede probably doubted the authenticity of their figures, and we suspect that the "ancient book" existed only in Geoffrey's imagination. What he did was to gather all the legends together, to serve the very useful purpose of being the fountain head from which the poets and writers of romance drew their inspiration. There are happenings in Greece and Rome, and Gaul and Britain. Leir and Cordeilla, Merlin and the magicians and Arthur all live in his pages.

126 Figure from the Gospels of St. Chad

We must now consider Manuscripts, because these writings on vellum were the means by which the literature of the time was given to the people.

The Anglo-Saxons were skilled penmen and artists; many of the beautiful manuscripts which they produced survive to this day. Books were precious objects, written by hand and illuminated by drawings which often have little or no relationship to the text but which merely enrich and beautify the pages. The first letters of a paragraph, for example, might be

127 David rescuing the lamb from the lion (*From a Psalter in St. John's College, Cambridge*)

contorted and twisted and perhaps embellished with a small animal head. A particularly magnificent initial X almost completely fills the page of the manuscript in fig. *132* and a series of small, yet delightful, initials are illustrated in fig. *124*. Sometimes, as in fig. *125*, the artist attempted to draw human and animal figures and, although he may not seem to have been very successful in representing them directly, he often caught the spirit of the fabulous animal he was portraying; the lion, for instance, in the top right-hand panel of fig. *133* has a very ferocious appearance.

Nobody knows when manuscripts were first painted in England, but as most writing was done by clerics we must presume that the introduction of Christianity at the end of the sixth century was responsible for the start of English writing and painting. But the earliest manuscript written in the British Isles that survives must date from about the middle of the seventh century. One of the finest works of art ever produced in this country was written and illuminated about fifty years later. It takes its name from the monastery in which it was made and is known as the Lindisfarne Gospels. The quality of the penmanship used in illuminating this book is so extremely fine that a modern artist would probably not be able to equal it. The brilliant colours of the interlaced animal ornament (some of which is shown in fig. *132*) are an impressive testimony to the skill of the Anglo-Saxon artist.

The tradition of fine illumination never completely died out in England, although during Alfred's reign and in the difficult years that followed few manuscripts survive which are of very

128   A border from the Gospels of Durrow

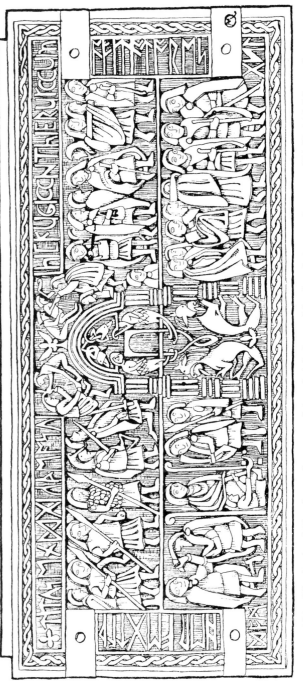

129 The back of Franks casket, carved in whale's bone. Northumbrian work, c. A.D. 700 (*British Museum*)

130 Reconstructed bone writing-tablet from Blythburgh, Suffolk (*British Museum*)

great quality. It was in this period that the practice of outline drawing was introduced into England from the Continent. This practice developed alongside the native tradition of fine coloured illumination throughout the tenth century. The English tradition of manuscript illumination can be seen to reach a new peak in the tenth century with the production of two important books (now in the British Museum): the Benedictional of St. Aethelwold and the Charter of the New Minster at Winchester. That this tradition continued in the period after the Norman Conquest can be seen from a group of manuscripts produced at Durham in the late eleventh century which are in direct descent from the earlier English manuscripts.

We have seen, on page 135, that Bede stated how, by the study of Scripture, the Latin tongue, and with it Roman characters, became common to the people; but there were others. A scramasax, or knife, at the British Museum is interesting because it has the Runic characters engraved on it. This system of writing was used by the Nordic peoples, and dates back to the fourth century, but was not in general use in England after the eighth. Its angular form made it very suitable for engraving on wood or stone.

Runes are cut on the wonderful Franks casket in the King Edward VII

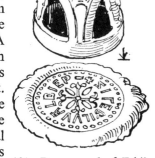

131 Bronze seal of Ethilwald, Bishop of Dunwich, about 850, from Eye, Suffolk (*British Museum*)

132 Page from Lindisfarne Gospels (*British Museum*)

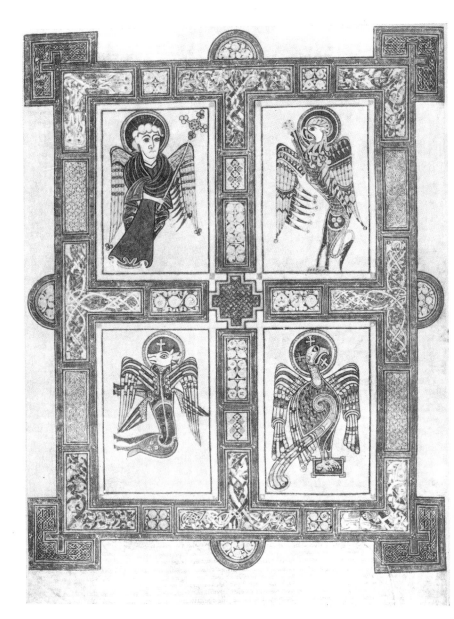

133 Page from the Book of Kells (*Trinity College, Dublin*)

BONE CARVING

Gallery at the British Museum(*129*), to explain the carvings, where Egil the archer is shown fighting his enemies; Wayland the smith makes a drinking-cup of a skull, and Romulus and Remus are with their foster-mother the Wolf. The casket is made of whalebone, and is Northumbrian work of about A.D. 700. It should be studied also for the details it gives of costume.

Another form of writing is that which employed the Ogham characters. These can be studied at the British Museum, and consisted of horizontal and diagonal strokes, and dots, grouped in series up to five, cut on the faces and edges of a tombstone for example. It is thought that the system was invented in Ireland.

The British Museum contains the only known example of a tenth century Anglo-Saxon writing-tablet(*130*) made of bone with sunk panels inside in which wax was spread to take the scratched writing done with a metal stylus.

Other writing was done with a reed, or quill pen, on the parchment of manuscripts or deeds. These were sealed with wax, by a bronze seal(*131*) which belonged to Ethilwald, Bishop of Dunwich, whose See, or seat, had long since been swallowed up by the waves.

At the Museum there is an impression of a seal, in lead, of Coenwulf, king of Mercia, 796–819. It was a *bulla* of lead like this, attached to papal documents, which gave rise to the name of papal "bulls".

We will consider now the great part which Christianity played in civilizing the English, but first we must endeavour to put ourselves in their places. We must remember that their faith had been much the same as that of the Vikings we describe on page 180, and an eminently suitable one for the warrior. By fighting he reached Valhal, and remained there. There were no complexities, or subtleties; the gods were destroyers like men. We must try and imagine their astonishment when Aidan, or Augustine, preached to them of the Sermon on the Mount, and told them that men were made in the image of God, and not a god like Woden, but a God of Love; that they could be creators. Here was a Faith which was easy to understand, and yet so difficult to live up to, because men continued, and still continue, to be more like the images of the old heathen gods they themselves had made.

134 Old timber-framed church at Urnes, Sogn, Norway. Eleventh century

We will trace all this in the pages of Bede, but first we must remember, as already stated on page 125, that the Britons were converted long before the Mission of St. Augustine, and that the Irish Church was in continuous descent from the Romano-British Church. There were differences between the Church of Ireland and that of Rome, mainly as to the proper date for keeping Easter, and these were not composed until the Synod of Whitby in 664. We must not think of Rome as the only source of Christian inspiration. When Christ was born, Rome, and Roman civilization, was at a low ebb, and it was not till the Edict of Toleration, in 313, that Christianity was recognized there. But Christ was born in Palestine, and here it was in Asia Minor that the greater part of the work of the Apostles was carried out. As a result, Christianity was adopted as the State religion at Edessa, in North Mesopotamia, as early as 202, and in

162

Armenia at the end of the century. Bede, in the first chapter of his history, compares England with Armenia, Macedonia, Italy, and other countries. This is very interesting, because Professor Strzygowski has shown that there are striking parallels between the church architecture of Asia Minor and that evolved here in England. The church at Silchester built here in Roman times (page 38) can be called Basilican, because it was founded on the Roman basilica, and the Saxon church of Worth, in Sussex, follows the same pattern and has an apse at the east end. If, however, we take Escomb, Durham, we find a different type of church with a square ended chancel. This latter type may have been introduced, not from Rome, but Asia Minor, and it is more usual in England than the apse. The question is were they influenced in their design by motives which travelled from Asia Minor to South Russia in the same way as the love of colour and jewellery to which we referred on page 124. Many of the Saxon churches give the idea of timber designs carried out in stone and they brought a timber building tradition with them.

Some of the early churches must have been on the lines of the old Norwegian timber church(*134*). We deal more fully with church architecture in the next chapter.

The practice of building wayside crosses seems to have started in Saxon times. These marked the way, or the parting of the ways, or where the river could be forded, or, as a nun writing in 699, said,

135   Ornament, Urnes Church

it is customary among the Saxon people, on the estates of the nobles or gentry, to have for the use of those who make a point of attending daily prayers, not a church, but the sign of the Holy Cross, set up aloft and consecrated to the Lord.

163

Augustine came to England in 597, at the instigation of Bertha, daughter of the king of the Franks, and wife of Ethelbert, king of Kent. We shall let Bede tell the tale:

> On the east of Kent is the large Isle of Thanet, containing, according to the English way of reckoning, 600 families. [Augustine stayed until] Some days after, the king came into the island, and sitting in the open air, ordered Augustine and his companions to be brought into his presence. For he had taken precaution that they should not come to him in any house, lest, according to an ancient superstition, if they practised any magical arts, they might impose upon him, and so get the better of him.

As a result of his preaching, Augustine was allowed to settle at Canterbury, where

> there was on the east side of the city, a church dedicated to the honour of St. Martin, built whilst the Romans were still in the island, wherein the queen, who, as has been said before, was a Christian, used to pray. In this they first began to meet, to sing, to pray, to say mass, to preach and to baptize, till the king, being converted to the faith, allowed them to preach openly, and build or repair churches in all places.

The Roman St. Martin's appears to have consisted of a plain oblong chapel, with a semi-circular apse of which little remains now, because the western end of the present chancel was the eastern end of the original chapel, and the apse lies under the floor where the building has been extended. Bede shows that at the time of Augustine, there must have been many other Romano-British churches.

The sudden conversion of great multitudes of people presented difficulty when they came to be baptized. Baptism was by total immersion, and as Bede tells us, "for as yet oratories, or fonts, could not be made in the early infancy of the church in these parts", so the grown-up converts flocked to the rivers and were baptized there.

One of the sites associated with Paulinus's mission to Northumbria is Yeavering in Northumberland, a place we described briefly on page 139. Here in 627 at the request of King Edwin Paulinus spent a number of days baptizing the people in the neighbourhood.

We can imagine Paulinus preaching to the pagans and newly

converted Christians from the rostrum of the moot (or meeting-place), the plan of which was uncovered by Mr Hope-Taylor: it had a triangular plan with a curved short side (not unlike a wedge of cake) with a rostrum at the apex. The seats rose from the rostrum in tiers so that the whole audience was able to see the speaker clearly.

There is a beautiful passage in Bede, dealing with the conversion of Edwin of Northumbria, in 625, by Paulinus, who was

> tall of stature, a little stooping, his hair black, his visage meagre, his nose slender and aquiline, his aspect both venerable and majestic. [He preached to the king, and Coifi, the chief priest, urged that the old gods be deserted] For none of your people has applied himself more diligently to the worship of our gods than I; and yet there are many who receive greater favours from you, and are more preferred than I, and are more prosperous in all their undertakings. Now if the gods were good for anything they would rather forward me, who have been more careful to serve them.

Here is a splendid illustration of the old pagan spirit of which we wrote on page 82; a bargain was made with the gods and, for the service rendered by worship, rewards were expected.

Another of the king's chief men was moved by Paulinus to a nobler strain, and said:

> The present life of man, O king, seems to me, in comparison of that time which is unknown to us, like to the swift flight of a sparrow through the room wherein you sit at supper in winter, with your commanders and ministers, and a good fire in the midst, whilst the storms of rain and snow prevail abroad; the sparrow, I say, flying in at one door, and immediately out at another, whilst he is within is safe from the wintry storm; but after a short space of fair weather, he immediately vanishes out of your sight, into the dark winter from which he had emerged. So this life of man appears for a short space, but of what went before, or what is to follow, we are utterly ignorant. If, therefore, this new doctrine contains something more certain, it seems justly to deserve to be followed.

This man was a poet.

Coifi, as a priest, could not carry arms and had to ride a mare, so when he threw off his allegiance to the old gods he begged for the king's stallion and arms, and girding on a sword and taking a spear, galloped to the temple and cast the spear into the temple and destroyed it; but then Coifi was not a poet, and this was just the ungrateful thing that a realist would do.

But all the temples were not destroyed in this way. Pope Gregory wrote to Abbot Mellitus, in 601, that

> the temples of the idols in that nation (English) ought not to be destroyed; but let the idols that are in them be destroyed; let holy water be made and sprinkled in the said temples, let altars be erected and relics placed.

We have already seen how one of these pagan temples, at Yeavering, was adapted to Christian use (page 139).

Again the Church was charitable. Pope Gregory pointed out that as the heathen English had "been used to slaughter many oxen in the sacrifices to devils, some solemnity must be exchanged for them on this account". Christianity was not to be made doleful. The festivals were to be feast days when the people could be festive. They were to be allowed "to build themselves huts of the boughs of trees, about those churches which have been turned to that use from temples, and celebrate the solemnity with religious feasting, and no more offer beasts to the Devil, but kill cattle to the praise of God in their eating".

So the good work continued until it looked as if the country were to see peace. We read that in the time of Edwin, King of Northumbria, "a woman with her new-born babe might walk throughout the island, from sea to sea, without receiving any harm. That king took such care for the good of his nation that in several places where he had seen clear springs near the highways he caused stakes to be fixed, with brass dishes hanging at them, for the convenience of travellers." But the fight was not won yet. Edwin was killed at the battle of Hatfield, by invading Mercians under Penda, who was still pagan. Paulinus fled to the south, and his work was largely undone.

Now we come to the very special service which the Church of Ireland rendered to the Christian cause. Oswald, the king who succeeded to the throne of Northumbria, had passed some part of his youth in the monastery of Iona, which, as we have seen on page 125, was founded by Columba, who went there from Ireland about 563, and it was to Iona that Oswald sent for help. They sent him, in 635, "Bishop Aidan, a man of singular meekness, piety, and moderation; zealous in the cause of God, though not altogether according to knowledge; for he was wont to keep Easter Sunday according to the custom of his country." This was the old quarrel.

Oswald appointed Aidan to his episcopal see in the Isle of Lindisfarne, which we call Holy Island for this reason, and he was successful in his work of reconversion. We read in Bede that many religious men and women, stirred by the example of Aidan, "adopted the custom of fasting on Wednesdays and Fridays, till the ninth hour, throughout the year, except during the fifty days after Easter". Later on, in 664, the differences between the two churches were composed, and Theodore "was the first archbishop whom all the English Church obeyed".

The conversion of the South Saxons occurred at an even later date. Bede tells how Bishop Wilfrid went to Sussex, in 681, and found the inhabitants in great distress. He baptized 250 men and women slaves, and "not only rescued them from the servitude of the Devil, but gave them their bodily liberty also, and exempted them from the yoke of human servitude".

He put heart into them. A dreadful famine ensued on three years drought, so that often

> forty or fifty men, being spent with want, would go together to some precipice, or to the seashore, and there, hand in hand, perish by the fall, or be swallowed up by the waves. [This was while they were heathen, because on the very day the nation was baptized rain fell. The bishops not only saved their souls, but] taught them to get their food by fishing; for their sea and rivers abounded in fish, but the people had no skill to take them, except eels alone. The bishop's men having gathered eel-nets everywhere, cast them into the sea, and by the blessing of God took three hundred fishes of several sorts.

Wilfrid founded a monastery at Selsey, the Island of the Sea-Calf. Earlier there had been a small monastery of Irish monks at Bosham, "but none of the natives cared either to follow their course of life, or hear their preaching".

The early Church was tremendously concerned in keeping its members to the true Faith, and it had to combat the heretics who would have divided it up into many small sects. Had this happened, the assault on heathendom would have failed, and with the failure the history of Western Europe would have been different. The Greek Church, which is a federation of many

167

eastern churches of which the most important is the Church of Russia, remained in communion with the Church of Rome until 1054.

Again the Church was compelled to interest itself in temporal affairs. The Popes wrote to the Kings, and urged them to lead Christian lives, and the Pope signed himself, "the servant of the servants of God". Pope Boniface, in 625, wrote to King Edwin, and sent him "a shirt, with one gold ornament, and one garment of Ancyra", and to Queen Ethelberga "a silver looking-glass, and gilt-ivory comb".

The bishops were rewarded. Pope Gregory sent the pallium to Augustine. The pallium was a long strip of fine woollen cloth, ornamented with crosses, the middle of which was formed with a loose collar resting on the shoulders, while the extremities before and behind hung down nearly to the feet.

136   Figure of Christ, in bronze. Irish (*British Museum*)

It would be well for us perhaps to try and catch a little of the spirit which animated these men in their fight, because it was as a fight against the powers of darkness that they regarded their work. If they held a Bible in one hand, in the other there was a sword.

Augustine summoned a conference, in 603, to which the bishops of the Britons were invited, and at which the date of Easter was discussed. Augustine wrought a miracle restoring a blind man's sight, after the British bishops had failed, to convince them that his church was in the right; but they remained unconvinced. Bede then tells how

> the man of God, Augustine, is said, in a threatening manner, to have foretold, that in case they would not join in unity with their

168

brethren, they should be warred upon by their enemies; and, if they would not preach the way of life to the English nation, they should at their hands undergo the vengeance of death.

This is what happened. The Britons were defeated by the English, at Chester, with great slaughter, and 1,200 monks from Bangor were among the slain. There was not much love lost between them. Even Bede refers to the Britons as "that perfidious nation".

Bede gives a beautiful vision of what the seventh-century man was given to expect after death. A Northumbrian rose from the dead, and related the things which he had seen.

He that led me had a shining countenance and a bright garment, and we went on silently, as I thought, towards the north-east. Walking on, we came to a vale of great breadth and depth, but of infinite length; on the left it appeared full of dreadful flames, the other side was no less horrid for violent hail and cold snow flying in all directions; both places were full of men's souls, which seemed by turns to be tossed from one side to the other, as it were by a violent storm; for when the wretches could no longer endure the excess of heat, they leaped into the middle of the cutting cold; and finding no rest there, they leaped back again into the middle of the unquenchable flames [the guide said] this is not the hell you imagine.

137 Figure in Bronze. Irish (*British Museum*)

They passed on to a place where

As we went on through the shades of night, on a sudden there appeared before us frequent globes of black flames, rising as it were out of a great pit, and falling back again into the same. When I had been conducted thither, my leader suddenly vanished, and left me alone in the midst of darkness and this horrid vision, whilst those same globes of fire, without intermission, at one time flew up and at another fell back into the bottom of the abyss; and I observed that all the flames, as they ascended, were full of human souls, which, like sparks flying up with smoke, were sometimes

169

138   The Ruthwell Cross (partial reconstruction). The cross is now inside
Ruthwell Church, Dumfriesshire

thrown on high, and again, when the vapour of the fire ceased, dropped down into the depth below.

Turning towards the south-east, and coming to the top of a vast wall, they found within it a delightful field, full of fragrant flowers. "In this field were innumerable assemblies of men in white, and many companies seated together rejoicing." The Northumbrian was told: "This is not the kingdom of heaven, as you imagine."
When he had passed farther on he

discovered before me a much more beautiful light, and therein heard sweet voices of people singing, and so wonderful a fragrancy proceeded from the place, that the other which I had before thought most delicious, then seemed to me very indifferent; even as that extraordinary brightness of the flowery field, compared with this, appeared mean and inconsiderable.

But beyond this they were not allowed to pass.
The guide then told the Northumbrian what were the places he had seen. The dreadful vale was the place "in which the souls of those are tried and punished, who, delaying to confess their crimes, at length have recourse to repentance at the point of death", but after punishment they were received into the Kingdom of Heaven.
The fiery pit was the mouth of Hell, "into which whosoever falls shall never be delivered to all eternity".
The first flowery field was the place for those who were

not so perfect as to deserve to be immediately admitted into the Kingdom of Heaven; yet they shall all, at the day of judgment, see Christ, and partake of the joys of His kingdom; for whoever are perfect, in thought, word and deed, as soon as they depart the body, immediately enter into the Kingdom of Heaven; in the neighbourhood whereof that place is, where you heard the sound of sweet singing, with the fragrant odour and bright light.

Chapter VI

THE COMING OF THE VIKINGS

So far as this part is concerned, we shall deal with the history of our country, between 815, when the Britons were finally conquered by the Saxons under Ecgberht, King of Wessex, up to the final conquest of the Saxons by the Danes under Canute in 1016, and then on to the Norman Invasion in 1066.

In the Saga of Burnt Njal is told the story of a Viking warrior who joined forces with Hallvard the White and went to seek his fortune away from his family and homeland. The name of this warrior was Gunnar and he was typical of many men from Scandinavia in the period between the eighth and eleventh centuries. Gunnar and those like him were pirates and their names indicate their character: Eric Bloodaxe, Harold Wartooth, Wolf the Unwashed, and Thorkell the Skull-splitter. They were tough pirates who plundered and burnt their way across Europe, from the Mediterranean to the North Atlantic, from the Caspian Sea to St. George's Channel, leaving a trail of devastation in their wake.

It was not till 787 that the Vikings turned their attention to this country. We read in the Anglo-Saxon Chronicle, that in this year

> first came three ships of Northmen, out of Haerethaland (Denmark). And then the reve (sheriff) rode out to the place, and would have driven them to the King's town, because he knew not who they were: and they there slew him. These were the first ships of Danishmen who sought the land of the English nation.

"God's church at Lindisfarne" was destroyed in 793, and Jarrow 794. There appear to have been two lines of attack. The first was from the Danes and Gotas who lived around the Wick, or Vik, now the fjord of Oslo. A glance at the map will show how easily they could come south by hugging the shore, and then crossing to the Thames, work down the Channel. The second line was from Norway to Shetland, and then south on either side of Scotland, to Northumbria on one hand, and Ireland on the other.

The Vikings occupied Ireland for about two centuries, and were differentiated there, because the Norsemen were known as the white strangers (*Finn-Gaill*), and the Danes as the dark strangers (*Dubh-Gaill*).

We know all these things; they are the commonplaces of history. What we do not really understand is how it came about that this Northern people should in the first place have felt the tremendous necessity for movement, and then have been so well equipped that they were able to carry out their schemes.

There were probably many reasons why the Vikings left their homeland in Scandinavia and went plundering in all parts of the known world. Some went out as pirates for the simple reason that they wanted money, some went in search of land, some to escape the law, or the displeasure of the King, and some because they were adventurers and were restless. Some went as traders and the great ports of the Viking world—Birka, near the modern Stockholm; Hedeby, near the modern Slesvig; Shiringshal, near the modern Kaupang in Norway—were important merchant centres as well as meeting-places for the Viking pirates. And although there can be little doubt as to the rapacious character of the Vikings, it is as well to remember that their doings were recorded by their enemies in extremely unfavourable terms and that it was the Vikings who introduced the word "Law" into the English language.

Three ships came in 787, but in 833 as many as 35 came to Charmouth and, by 851, 350 came to the mouth of the Thames. We cannot follow all their movements here, but Wales, Ireland, and France were all raided. One important detail is that Rurik, King of Sweden, founded the kingdom of Russia at the end of the ninth century. In this way the Vikings reached Kief, and from here went to take service with the Emperor at Constantinople, and fought in Asia Minor against the Saracens.

Harald Sigurdsson, son of Sigurd Syr, King of Norway, did this, and later became King of Norway as Harald Haardraade. Always something seems to happen when the Northern peoples rub shoulders with the old civilizations of the Near East. The Vikings brought back with them the rarest of commodities, ideas, and we have to admit that they were an extraordinary people.

Roman power was based on the legionary, but the Viking was the first to realize the meaning of sea-power. Their ships were beautifully designed and very speedy, so when they sailed up the rivers conveniently arranged for them on our East Coast, they took horses, put their webbed feet in stirrups, and rode through the country. They were like evil will-o'-the-wisps, never where the Saxons expected to find them. The English ceorl, called up by the fyrd of the shire, was thinking of his crops, and armed only with spear and shield, was opposed to the Viking with steel cap and ring-mail shirt, who, as a mounted infantry man, could deliver his blow when, and where he liked.

This will be a good place in which to write of the Viking ship. If we turn back the pages of history we find how often some new idea has revolutionized the lives and liberties of the peoples. Armour, the bow, horse, military engineering, and the walled city, were all used in warfare long before the days of Christ. The Vikings had the wonderful ship which the stormy waters and the seafaring genius of their people had developed to perfection. We know what these were like, because the old Vikings loved their boats so well that they were buried in them. We saw on page 136 how in *Beowulf* the dead Scyld was placed in his ship, and pushed off to sail away into the unknown. In another type of funeral the body was placed in the ship and both burned together. A third type is more useful to the archaeologists, because here the ship was pulled up on to land, and the dead body placed in it, with all the articles which the warrior would need in the spirit world. Then over the whole a barrow of earth was piled to remain for excavation in our time.

It was a beautiful idea and shows how the Viking loved his ship: in the Sagas he calls it the "Reindeer of the breezes", the "Horse of gull's track", the "Raven of the wind", and many other equally poetic names.

Shall we conjure up the burial scene? The ship drawn up, its prow pointing to the sea; a salt breeze blowing in, stinging the nostrils and singing in the rigging. The procession from the hall, the dead Viking borne by his warriors, the body stiff and

139   On board the Gokstad ship

cold but dressed and armed for his last voyage. Then the slaughter of the terrified horses and whimpering dogs who were to accompany their master. Overhead, attracted by the smell of blood, the wheeling, screaming gulls, like valkyries sent by Odin as an escort to Valhalla. Some such scene was staged around the ship illustrated in figs. *139* and *140*. These illustrations have been drawn from the boat discovered at Gokstad, near Sandefjord on Oslofjord in Norway.

The ship was clinker built, with overlapping planks of oak. About 78 feet long, her beam was 16 feet 7 inches, and depth 6 feet 9 inches. She had more beam than is generally imagined (*140*). The one square sail was useful before the wind, and at other times there were sixteen oars for pulling on each side. The mast was stepped as shown in fig. *139*, and kept in position by a heavy slab dropped into a slot; it was lowered aft by slacking off the forestay. The vessel was steered by an oar at a point near the stern. The lines of hull were as beautiful as those of a modern yacht, and just as scientifically modelled, so as to offer the minimum resistance to the passage through the water. At night a tilt was put up (*140*). Fig. *141* shows one of the wooden beds found on the Gokstad ship. Made of oak, it is ingeniously constructed so that it could be taken to pieces. The posts are

SECTION AMIDSHIPS.

140   The Gokstad ship with tilt up

2 feet 3 inches high; the ends 3 feet 5 inches wide, and the sides 7 feet 5 inches long. Only the chiefs would have had beds. Another Viking boat was recovered from Oseberg, not far from

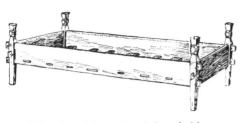

141   A bed from the Gokstad ship

Gokstad. This was the burial ship of a queen and contained finely carved furniture and many implements and ornaments, some of which had been brought by the Vikings from England.

There is a note in William of Malmesbury bearing on boats. Godwin gave Hardicanute

> a ship beaked with gold, having eighty soldiers on board, who had two bracelets on either arm, each weighing sixteen ounces of gold; on their heads were gilt helmets; on their left shoulder they carried a Danish axe, with an iron spear in their right hand.

The Anglo-Saxon Chronicle (891) gives details of other boats in use at the time of far more primitive build—"And three Scots (Irish) came to King Alfred in a boat without any oars from Ireland, whence they had stolen away. . . . The boat in which they came was made of two hides and a half." This sounds like a sea-curragh made of wicker and covered with hide as the coracle. The curragh is still in use on the west coast of Ireland. Tarred canvas on a light wooden frame replaces the animal skin. A rounder, smaller kind is used by fishermen on Welsh rivers.

We can now return to the doings of the Vikings on land. Asser tells a tale which shows that the Saxons credited them with supernatural powers.

> They say, moreover, that in every battle, wherever that flag went before them, if they were to gain the victory a live crow would appear flying in the middle of the flag; but if they were doomed to be defeated it would hang down motionless, and this was often proved so.

When they came to settle in the land, after the Peace of Wedmore, in 878, they showed great judgment in the selection of their five strongholds or burgs. The Vikings knew the importance of transport and they selected points which could easily be reached by land or water. Lincoln was on the River Witham, at the junction of the Roman Fosse Way and Ermine Street; Stamford on Ermine Street, and the River Welland; Leicester on the Fosse Way, and the River Soar; Derby on the River Derwent, and Ryknield Street; and Nottingham on the Trent.

When the Vikings were established in the Danelaw, they doubtless sent for their wives and children, and settled to live peacefully in the fortified towns of their new country. The peaceful side of Viking life is indicated by the comb illustrated in fig. *112*. A runic inscription is scratched on the comb which reads in the language and letters of a Viking "Thorfastr made a good comb". But the Viking influence is most clearly to be seen in our language and in our place-names. We have already noticed that the word "law" is Scandinavian in origin and many Norse survivals are to be found in the dialects of Cumberland and Westmorland. To berry (*berja*, thresh); the boose (*báss*, cow-shed); galt (*galti*, a pig); garn (*garn*, yarn); handsel (*handsöl*, bargain), and many others. Similarly the termination -*by* to a place-name (as in Derby) is a sure sign that it was once a Viking settlement.

Where the Vikings settled, the land was divided into trithings, wapentakes, and carucates. In Domesday these measurements are applied to Nottingham, Leicester, Derby, Rutland, and Lincoln. Twelve carucates equal one hundred. The duodecimal, 12, seems to have come from the Dane, and the long hundred of 120 is a survival from their times. Another interesting detail is found in Domesday, where more freemen are mentioned in the Danelaw than elsewhere, and the men of that part still perhaps think of themselves as being sturdier in thought and action than their Saxon cousins of the South.

The names of the Things, or Assemblies, of which we read in Burnt Njal, survive in names like the Suffolk hundred of Thingoe, or Tinghowe, Tingewick, near Buckingham, and Tingrith, South Bedfordshire.

But if the arrival of the Vikings was an advantage in one way, in that it stiffened the fibre of the race, in another it was fraught

142 Font in Deerhurst Church, Gloucestershire. When set up again in the church the ornament of the base was placed immediately under the bowl

with great peril. When they first came, in 787, they were pagans and the delicate fabric of Christianity was torn down and trampled in the dust. Churches were destroyed, monasteries plundered, and the civilization of the country put back centuries.

Odin, Thor, and Frey were the greatest of their gods. Odin, the God of Wisdom, was the chief, and the same as the Anglo-Saxon Woden. Tall and bearded, he loved war, and his two ravens, Hugin and Munin, brought him news of men. He had only one eye, having sacrificed the other to drink wisdom at the Well of Mimir. As the Chief of the gods he had a hall, Valhal. The Valkyries were his attendants, and the choosers of the dead. Virgin goddesses, armed with helmet, shield and spear, and mounted on horseback, they rode through the air, over the rainbow, the celestial bridge which gods and men must tread to reach Valhalla. Only those who died in battle or who met a violent death were chosen, and taken back to feast with Odin, to find their pastime in fighting and their reward in that they always lived on to feast, and fight, another day. The sorry souls who died in their beds never reached Valhal, but went instead to *Hel.* Ty was the God of War, and Thor, the Thunder God, protected farmers and threw his hammer, which is the thunderbolt. The gods accepted the sacrifice of horses, oxen, sheep, and boars, but in times of great trouble their will was found by casting lots, and men were killed to appease them. This was the animating faith of the Vikings, who nearly conquered the world of their day, and whose blood still flows in English veins.

The period of this second part of our book was a tragic one for the Saxons in England, the gloom of which was only dispelled by the gallant stand made by Alfred. He turned his levy into a militia, part of which was always on duty; he fortified burgs and improved his fleet. He not only protected England in his time, but laid the foundations of a power which was to conquer her yet again in 1066. Some Vikings finding that Alfred's fleet really did mean business, turned their attention to Gaul, where they eventually settled down, in 912, founding Normandy.

The Franks did not find them particularly pleasant neighbours. William of Malmesbury tells how Charles, King of the Franks, finding that he could not beat the Normans, proposed to them that they should hold the land they had already conquered as his vassals. Rollo thought it over, and

> the inbred and untamed ferocity of the man may well be imagined, for, on receiving this gift, as the bystanders suggested to him that he ought to kiss the foot of his benefactor, disdaining to kneel down, he seized the king's foot and dragged it to his mouth as he stood erect. The king falling on his back, the Normans began to laugh, and the Franks to be indignant.

This is an interesting passage. History was repeating itself. Long years before, the Franks and Saxons had descended on the Gauls and Britons and treated them in much the same way; now they themselves were helpless before the Vikings. Just as the Gauls and Britons had learned to lean on the strong arm of Rome, and could not stand alone when it was withdrawn, so the Franks and Saxons found civilized life enervating.

We do not concern ourselves very much with the doings of kings, because generally they are so remote from everyday life, but this cannot be said of Alfred; perhaps that is why his name lives. Here was a king who, though kingly, had touched adversity and known trouble.

There are two tales which are well known, but explain why he had such a hold on his people. Asser tells one, of how when the king had taken refuge in a hut

> it happened on a certain day, that the countrywoman, wife of the cowherd, was preparing some loaves to bake, and the king, sitting at the hearth, made ready his bow and other warlike instruments. The unlucky woman espying the cakes burning at the fire, ran up to remove them,

and gave the king a little bit of her mind, telling him that if he wanted to eat the cakes, he might at least have watched them.

The other tale is told by William of Malmesbury, of the time when Alfred was hard pressed at Athelney:

> Not long after, venturing from his concealment, he hazarded an experiment of consummate art. Accompanied only by one of his most faithful adherents, he entered the tent of the Danish king under the disguise of a minstrel; and being admitted, as a professor of the mimic art, to the banqueting room there was no object of secrecy that he did not minutely attend to, both with eyes and ears.

These are typical legends of a type that commonly grows up around a great hero; they should not be taken too literally—

they are however indicative of the honour and affection in which Alfred was held by the English.

But even Alfred's genius could only maintain a hold on the south-west of England, and by the Peace of Wedmore, 878, Northumbria, half of Mercia, and East Anglia became the Danelaw. We must find out more about Alfred because, if we obtain a picture of the Saxons at their best from Bede, under Alfred and his immediate descendants they made a good fight before they were swamped by the Danes.

Asser the historian, who lived at the court of Alfred, tells us that he "remained illiterate even till he was twelve years old or more; but he listened with serious attention to the Saxon poems which he often heard recited". His father Ethelwulf sent him to Rome, in 853, and took him there again in 855. Notwithstanding the advantages of foreign travel, as late as 884 "he had not yet learned to read anything".

When Alfred became king, he paid great attention to education. He imported Johannes Scotus from France to assist, but the schoolboys do not seem to have taken to him kindly, because we are told that he "was pierced with the iron styles of the boys he was instructing".

Alfred did not suffer from his own lack of schooling, because we read that he "was affable and pleasant to all, and curiously eager to investigate things unknown". This being the case, the king determined to acquire knowledge, and then pass it on to his subjects. He realized that History, to be of any real use to a people, must have an international flavour about it, and not be too self-consciously national; nations are like individuals and must rub shoulders.

Alfred therefore took "The History of the World, from the Creation to 416", by Orosius, a Spaniard, and caused it to be translated into Anglo-Saxon, and while this was being done he inserted accounts of the travels of two of his contemporaries, Ohthere, and Wulfstan.

Ohthere was a Norseman, who following the adventurous habit of his people, had come to England, and had visited the Saxon Court.

Ohthere told his lord, King Alfred, that he dwelt northmost of all Northmen. [He was one of the first explorers.] He said that, at a certain time, he wished to find out how far the land lay right north; or whether any man dwelt to the north of the waste. Then he went right north near the land; he left, all the way, the waste land on the right, and the wide sea on the left, for three days. Then was he as far north as whale-hunters ever go. He then went yet right north, as far as he could sail in the next three days. Then the land bent there right east, or the sea in on the land, he knew not whether; but he knew that he there waited for a western wind, or a little to the north, and sailed thence east near the land, as far as he could sail in four days. Then he must wait there for a right north wind, because the land bent there right south, or the sea in on the land, he knew not whether. Then sailed he thence right south, near the land, as far as he could sail in five days.

Ohthere had rounded the North Cape, and reached the White Sea. He found the Biarmians living on the shore there, and hunted horse-whales (walruses), "because they have very good bone in their teeth . . . and their hides are very good for ship-ropes."

Ohthere was a wealthy man in his own country, having 600 reindeer, 20 horned cattle, 20 sheep, and 20 swine.

Alfred's interest in sea-power and his realization of its importance is illustrated by the well-known passage in the Anglo-Saxon Chronicle:

> Then King Alfred commanded long-ships to be built to oppose the esks; they were full nigh twice as long as the others; some had sixty oars, and some had more; they were both swifter and steadier, and also higher than the others. They were shapen neither like the Frisian nor the Danish, but so as it seemed to him they would be most efficient.

Unfortunately they were not very efficient vessels and were little use against the skilfully handled Viking ships.

Alfred was a great builder in other ways. He repaired London in 886. This raises a very interesting problem. Did he repair and rebuild London in the Roman manner? In Alfred's time there must have been many buildings which were nearly perfect, and he may have restored these. This is suggested by Asser, who wrote, "What shall I say of the cities and towns which he restored . . . of the royal vills constructed of stone, removed from their old site, and handsomely rebuilt." The Saxons would not have been able to originate a classical building, but they may have restored them. In any picture then of Saxon

London, side by side with their timber halls, we must be prepared for these old Roman buildings given a new lease of life by Alfred's genius.

Asser tells how he encouraged people "to build houses, majestic and good, beyond all the precedents of his ancestors, by his new mechanical inventions". Whether these were wood or stone we do not know, but he built a church at Athelney on what was regarded as a new plan. He planted four posts in the ground, which formed the angles of the main structure, and around these built four aisles. This must have resembled the old Norwegian timber-framed church shown in fig. *134*, and was not at all classical, but entirely northern in conception.

A note in the Anglo-Saxon Chronicle (978) on houses suggests that the hall had been moved up to what we should now call the first floor level, where it was to remain until the fourteenth century—

> In this year all the chief "Witan" of the English nation fell at Calne from an upper chamber, except the holy archbishop Dunstan, who alone supported himself upon a beam.

Neither houses nor churches were very comfortable. Asser tells how the king caused 6 candles to be made out of 72 pennyweights of wax; each candle had 12 divisions and lasted 4 hours, so that the 6 candles lasted through the 24 hours. But owing to the "violence of the wind, which blew day and night without intermission through the doors and windows of the churches", the candles guttered and did not keep correct time, so the king "ordered a lantern to be beautifully constructed of wood and white ox-horn".

With the candles, Alfred "so divided the twenty-four hours of the day and night as to employ eight of them in writing, in reading, and in prayer, eight in the refreshment of his body, and eight in dispatching the business of his realm".

He had need to safeguard his time in this way, because there was so much for him to do. Laws had to be made. William of Malmesbury, in the throes of extreme hero-worship, tells us how Alfred

> appointed centuries, which they call "hundreds", and decennaries, that is to say, "tythings", so that every Englishman living, according to law, must be a member of both. If anyone was accused of a

crime, he was obliged immediately to produce persons from the hundred and tything to become his surety; and whosoever was unable to find such surety, must dread the severity of the laws. If any who was impleaded made his escape either before or after he had found surety, all persons of the hundred and tything paid a fine to the king. By this regulation he diffused such peace through the country, that he ordered golden bracelets, which might mock the eager desires of the passengers while no one durst take them away, to be hung up on the public causeways, where the roads crossed each other.

The personal combat was another method of settling differences. In 1041, we read of William Malmesbury, that Gunhilda, sister of Hardecanute, and wife of Henry, Emperor of the Germans, was accused of adultery—

> She opposed in single contest to her accuser, a man of gigantic size, a young lad of her brother's establishment, whom she had brought from England, while her other attendants held back in cowardly apprehension. When, therefore, they engaged, the impeacher, through the miraculous interposition of God, was worsted, by being ham-strung.

Alfred appears to have been content to concentrate the power of Wessex within its own borders, and it was left to his successors to carry war into the Danelaw. They were so successful, that under Eadred, and then Eadgar, with the assistance of Dunstan, the Danelaw submitted, and England became one kingdom; then came decline, and by the days of Aethelred the Unready, 978–1016, the whole of England passed into Danish hands. The dismal tale can be traced in the Chronicle. In that year (991) it was decreed that tribute, for the first time, should be given to the Danish men, on account of the great terror which they caused by the sea coast; that was at first 10,000 pounds. In 994 it was 16,000, and in 1002, 24,000 pounds of money.

In 1005 "was the great famine throughout the English nation; such, that no man ever before recollected one so grim". 1009 was a tragic year. A navy had been built by a levy, "from three hundred hides and from ten hides, one vessel; and from eight hides, a helmet and a coat of mail". The ships were brought together at Sandwich but the whole business was wrecked by treachery and incapacity and "they let the whole nation's toil thus lightly pass away" so that when the Danes came again they ravaged and plundered as before, the people of East Kent paying 3000 pounds. "Then the king commanded the whole nation to be called out; so that they should be opposed on every side: but lo! nevertheless, they marched as they pleased."

The Chronicle contains a terrible picture of the death of Saxon Archbishop Elphege at the hands of the Danes. "And there they then shamefully slaughtered him: they cast upon him bones and the horns of oxen, and then one of them struck him with an axe-iron on the head, so that with the blow he sank down." But enough of Destruction. We will turn to the more pleasant task of writing of Construction, and fortunately for us, in the days between Alfred and Dunstan, there is an ample store of material on which to draw.

This will be a convenient place in which to discuss church buildings. Fig. *143* is the plan, and fig. *144* the interior of Wing Church, Buckinghamshire. On page 38 it will be seen that the Christian Church which was built at Silchester was called basilican, because it resembled the Basilica, or Hall of Justice, there. This Roman tradition of building was adopted at Wing, but the apse is polygonal, instead of being semi-circular as at Silchester. We think it is later than the nave, and fig. *145* shows how the exterior has the narrow strips of stone, which are characteristic of some Saxon buildings. The apse covers the crypt, or confessio, where a saintly man was buried, and this was so arranged that it could be seen into from the nave, and from openings on the outside. These crypts developed from the practice of worshipping in the catacombs at Rome at the graves of the early martyrs.

Fig. *147* shows a window opening at Wing, with the curious mid-wall shaft, which was the forerunner of the traceried window. The next step is shown in fig. *173.*

Fig. *146,* of Worth Church, Sussex, shows another Saxon church of basilican

143   Plan of Wing Church, Buckinghamshire

144 The interior of Wing Church (partial reconstruction)

type, with an apsidal east end. In the typical basilica, the bishop's chair stood in the centre of the apse, and the clergy sat on a bench around the wall. The altar stood on the chord of the apse. The choir was in front of the altar, with the catechumens, or those who were being instructed, in the nave. The women sat in one aisle, the men in the other, and the penitents in the porch.

Figs. *150, 152,* of the Saxon church at Bradford-on-Avon, Wiltshire, show the type of plan with a square ended chancel, which was to become the more usual English type of church.

145   East end of Wing Church (partial reconstruction)

146   Worth, Sussex

This church is one of the earliest churches known in the south of England. It was founded by Aldhelin at the end of the seventh century and was later reconstructed in the tenth century.

When the Saxons first began to build in stone, they imitated many of the details of timber buildings. This is very apparent in the tower at Earls Barton, Northamptonshire(*151*). Great

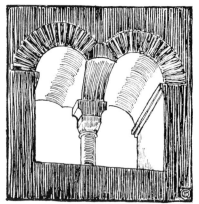

147 A window at Wing Church

care was taken here to cut back the masonry, so that only the narrow strips of stone were visible, and the walls between were plastered. The angle quoins, built with alternate long and short stones, are another typical Saxon detail. The towers of Saxon churches appear to have been used to house the sacristans on the first floor, to which access was gained by a wooden ladder. There were openings in the east wall of the tower which enabled the sacristan to keep watch over the church.

In the basilican churches the porch, or narthex, at first extended right across the width of the church(14). Later it was abbreviated into a western porch and this was then raised into a tower. Fig. 153 shows the tower doorway at Earls Barton, and how one of the stone strips was curved around it. Fig. 154, of the tower arch at St. Benet's Church, Cambridge, from the nave, shows this same detail on a larger scale, as well as the opening over it from which the sacristan could look down into the church from his room in the tower.

Fig. 155 shows the very fine tower arch at Sompting, Sussex, and fig. 156, of the exterior, is interesting as it is the only Saxon tower in England which has its original form of roof.

The ordinary churches were timber built. Edwin

148 Worth: Nave windows

190

149   Sculpture at Bradford-on-Avon Church

150   Interior of Bradford-on-Avon Church

was baptized at York in 627 in the Church of St. Peter the Apostle, which he himself had built of timber . . . but as soon as he was baptized, he took care by the direction of the same Paulinus, to build in the same place a larger and nobler church of stone, in the midst whereof that same oratory which he had first erected should be enclosed.

So the wooden oratory was the forerunner of the present cathedral.

Bells were used in churches. Bede tells how a nun on the night of St. Hilda's death, "on a sudden heard the well-known

151   Tower of Earls Barton Church, Northamptonshire
(partial reconstruction)

152 (*above*) Exterior of Bradford-on-Avon Church, Wiltshire

153 Tower doorway, Earls Barton Church

154 St. Benet's Church, Cambridge: tower arch

Sompting · Sussex
Tower arch
June '65 CHB.

155   Tower arch, Sompting Church, Sussex

156 Tower of Sompting Church

sound of a bell in the air, which used to awake and call them to prayers".

The British Museum possesses an interesting relic in the iron bell of St. Cuilleann, which was enshrined in bronze in the eleventh century. Evidently the early saints used ordinary cow-bells to summon their people, and these later became sacred relics. Their walking-sticks were treasured, and cased in metal became the type for the pastoral staff of a bishop.

Lack of space prevents us from dealing more fully with church architecture. The sketches we have given are sufficient to show that the art of the Saxon builder was sturdy and vigorous, and as the greater part of it is found in the Eastern and Midland counties, some of the credit must be given to the Danes and Vikings who settled in these parts. It should be remembered that we have to judge the builders by their smaller churches; the larger cathedrals were pulled down and rebuilt by the Normans.

Christianity meant the introduction of a new set of symbols into the world; these were very necessary when many people could not read. Heraldry was a form of symbolism, and also the later tradesmen's signs. The Church used the fish as a symbol of the Saviour, because the initials of the Greek words for "Jesus Christ, Son of God, Saviour" form the Greek word for fish. The Church was shown as a ship in which the faithful sailed safely across the sea of life, and Hope was typified as an

157 Head of Tau. Crozier of walrus ivory, found at Alcester, Warwickshire. Early eleventh century (*British Museum*)

158 St. Mark   159 St. Matthew

160 St. Luke   161 St. Mark

162 St. Mark   163 St. John

SYMBOLS OF THE EVANGELISTS
(158–61, 163 *from the Gospels of St. Chad*; 162 *from the Gospels of Durrow*)

anchor. Christ was the Good Shepherd, and the Devil a serpent. The soul of the departed was shown as a dove, and Victory as a palm branch; Immortality by a peacock; the Resurrection by the phoenix, and the soul thirsting for baptism as a stag. The triangle was the Trinity. The sacred monogram, or Chi-Rho, was formed of the first two letters of the Greek word for Christ. The Cross itself was used as a symbol in varying forms. The Tau(*157*), from the Greek character T; the St. Andrew's Cross like the Latin numeral X; the Latin Cross with the longer lower limb. The Evangelists each had their symbols: the Angel for St. Matthew, the Lion for St. Mark, the Ox for St. Luke and the Eagle for St. John(*158–63*).

Monasticism was introduced into this country in Saxon times. The practice was first begun by the anchorites, who in Egypt, in the third century, withdrew to the desert to pass their life in solitude and devotion. St. Pachomius organized them into a community at Tabennisi, near Denderah, 315–20, and this led to the Coptic and Abyssinian churches. The next development was in Syria, early in the fourth century, and, in the latter half, St. Basil, of Caesarea, instituted a system in Cappadocia. About 500, St. Benedict founded the great system, which bears his name, at the monastery of Monte Cassino, between Rome and Naples, which was to exercise so enormous an influence. Here in England, in Saxon times, the Rule was not followed with great strictness. In the Irish monasteries the monks, when at home, lived in separate cells, and when abroad preached the Gospel as missionaries. In the Benedictine monastery, the monks lived, prayed, and slept together in common. They were celebrated for their learning, and built fine churches; they cultivated the waste lands and were good farmers; they gave shelter to the scholar and the artist, and in a rough and turbulent age the cloak of religion was a better protection than the sword.

Here is the rent which the Abbot of Medeshamstede (Peterborough) charged for land that he let to Wilfred,

each year should deliver into the minster sixty loads of wood, and twelve of coal and six of faggots, and two tuns full of pure ale, and two beasts fit for slaughter, and six hundred loaves, and ten measures of Welsh ale, and each year a horse and thirty shillings, and one day's entertainment.

COINS AND TAX

This is an interesting passage because it shows that, though the usual method of trade was to barter commodities, yet money was in use as a means of exchange.

The Sceatta currency, and the Northumbrian styca, came before the penny first struck by Offa of Mercia. Many hoards of Anglo-Saxon coins have been discovered in this country, the most important being the find made in 1840, in a leaden chest near a ford over the Ribble, above Preston. It contained 10,000 silver coins, and nearly 1000 ozs of silver; it was buried between 903 and 905 and may have been the treasure chest of a Danish army. Coins have been found at Rome of Offa, 757–96, and may have been "Peter's Pence". Many more Anglo-Saxon coins have been found in Sweden than have been found in England. These Scandinavian finds presumably represent part of the Dane-geld —the tax paid by the English to buy off the Viking raiders. At the same time the presence of these coins in Scandinavia is a tribute to the high standard of the English coinage, for at this time the coinage of England was superior in quality and uniformity to any in Europe.

Church dues were a very heavy charge on industry in these early days. Canute wrote to Ethelnoth, to take care that

> all dues owing to ancient custom be discharged: that is to say, plough-alms (a penny to the poor for as much land as a plough could till), the tenth of animals born in the current year, and the pence owing to Rome for St. Peter; and in the middle of August the tenth of the produce of the earth; and on the festival of St. Martin, the first fruits of the seeds (a sack of corn from every load), to the church and the parish where each one resides.

People complain of high taxation in these days, but here was an Income Tax, not on the profit of the year, but the whole turn-over.

The Church gave very good value for the money received, because not only were the souls of the people saved, but their everyday life was regulated. Dunstan observed that

> as his countrymen used to assemble in taverns, and when a little elevated quarrel as to the proportion of their liquor, he ordered gold or silver pegs to be fastened in the pots, that whilst every man

knew his just measure, shame should compel each neither to take more himself nor oblige others to drink beyond their proportional share.

The Church at an early date encouraged pilgrimage. We read in the Chronicle (816): "The same year the English School at Rome was burned." This was near St. Peter's, for the accommodation of pilgrims. These pilgrimages played their part in educating and interesting people, and as the Church of Rome has always been very democratic, the son of a peasant could become first priest, then prelate, and, going to Rome, come back and tell his friends of all the fine things he had seen there. It is interesting to note, however, that many Anglo-Saxon craftsmen lived in Rome and that Anglo-Saxon metalworkers, working in Rome, supplied some of the sacred vessels for St. Peter's itself.

Aelfric is another of the churchmen who have left us a picture of Saxon times. He was a monk in the New Minster (Winchester), founded in the time of Eadgar (958–75). He tells of the ranks into which the people were divided, and it is evident that by his time there was less freedom than there had been. We have seen how in Alfred's time it became necessary to put the safety of the State before the comfort of the people. Formerly the main division was between "eorles" and "ceorles", or gentle

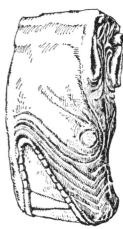

and simple, but if the "ceorl" thrived and had five hides of land, a church, kitchen, and a place in the king's hall, then he became worthy of Thane-right, and so could the merchant and the thane become an "eorl".

Aelfric, in his "Colloquies", tells us of the duties of men, and these by the time of Canute had been so regulated, that every man had his job and definite position in the State. The thegn held his land on condition that he rendered military service, and undertook the repair of fortifications, and bridge building. The geneat, cottar, and gebur were retainers, or tenants, of the thegn, or lord, and held their land on condition

164 Carving at Deerhurst Church, Gloucestershire

200

165   Funeral of Edward the Confessor (Bayeux tapestry)

that they supported him. The beekeeper, swineherd, oxherd, cowherd, shepherd, goatherd, cheesemaker, barnman, beadle, woodward, hayward, and the sowers all had their dues and duties defined. The keepers of animals had to guard them as well. Edgar "commanded Judwall, king of the Welsh, to pay him yearly a tribute of three hundred wolves". The slaves were not forgotten. A slave woman was entitled to eight pounds of corn for food, one sheep or three pennies for winter food, one sester of beans for Lenten fare, and in summer whey, or one penny. As well they were entitled to a feast at Christmas, and another at Easter, and a handful of corn at harvest beside their other dues. We do not know if Canute himself laid down these rules. In them it is stated that though customs varied, those mentioned were the general ones, yet if better could be found they would be gladly approved.

In viewing these customs ourselves we must not condemn them too hastily as having been based on slavery. The system was very closely knit and strong because it was based on the land. Our own world, for little more than a century (which, historically speaking, is only a flicker of time) has toyed with the ideas of freedom and liberty, and an industrial system which is weak because it is divorced from the land. Today whole classes of people are dependent on others for their schooling and books; have to be assisted to build houses, and have baths, and receive doles when they are unemployed, and subsidies when trade is bad. And we import nearly all our food. If Canute could have contrasted our customs with his own he might not have been greatly chagrined.

Perhaps the final note in this part should be one on the spread of knowledge which made possible the developments of the next period. William of Malmesbury tells of the training of Pope Silvester (1002), who travelled among the Saracens in the South of Spain. He practised the use of the astrolabe for making celestial observations, became skilled in astronomy and astrology; he acquired the art of calling up spirits from hell —arithmetic, music, and geometry; learned to use the abacus or counting table. Later in Gaul, when Archbishop of Rheims, he constructed a clock on "mechanical principles, and an hydraulic organ, in which the air, escaping in a surprising manner, by the force of heated water, fills the cavity of the instrument, and the brazen pipes emit modulated tones through the multifarious apertures".

Chapter VII

THE COMING OF THE NORMANS

I N this chapter we arrive at the period with which we start in Volume I of *A History of Everyday Things in England.* In that book we deal with the appearance of the Norman people and their ships, castles, monasteries, cathedrals, games, and general customs. We shall not, therefore, cover the same ground again, but seek for new types so that the two books may be complementary one to the other.

We think that the more the Normans are studied the greater respect one has for their energy and intelligence, but it needs some explanation why so much became possible to them. They were of the same Nordic type as the Saxons and Vikings, and it was as the Northmen, or Norsemen, that they settled in Normandy, under Hrolf, in 912, and, as we showed on page 180, very unpleasant neighbours the French found them.

We will now try to find out what kind of people they were. Our principal authority will be Master Wace and his Chronicle of the Norman Conquest from the Roman de Rou. Wace was a trouvère or troubadour at the court of Henry II, and his sprightly tale forms an admirable text to the pictures of the tapestry at Bayeux, which is another great record of the Conquest.

Wace gives us a graphic picture of life in Normandy when William was forging the sword with which to conquer England. His barons were turbulent, and before they could be welded into a whole by feudalism had to be persuaded to leave off killing one another. The Truce of God was introduced by William, in 1061, and enforced by him as a restraint on the Normans.

He made all swear on the relics to hold peace and maintain it from sunset on Wednesday to sunrise on Monday. This was called the TRUCE, and the like of it I believe is not in any country. If any man should beat another meantime, or do him any mischief, or take any of his goods, he was to be excommunicated, and amerced nine livres to the bishop.

Harold, on his way to Normandy, was taken prisoner by the Count of Ponthieu, and delivered up to William, who thus appeared to come to Harold's rescue. He was nobly entertained by the duke, and then trapped into promising to deliver England to the Norman on the death of Edward. To receive the oath, William caused a Parliament to be called. As well,

> He sent for all the holy bodies thither, and put so many of them together as to fill a whole chest, and then covered them with a pall; but Harold neither saw them, nor knew of them being there; for nought was shown or told to him about it; and over all was a phylactery, the best that he could select; œil de bœuf, I have heard it called. When Harold placed his hand upon it, the hand trembled and the flesh quivered; but he swore and promised upon his oath to take Ele to wife, and to deliver up England to the duke . . . when Harold . . . had risen upon his feet, the duke led him up to the chest, and made him stand near it; and took off the chest the pall that had covered it, and shewed Harold upon what holy relics he had sworn, and he was sorely alarmed at the sight.

We can read in Wace how, when Harold failed to keep his promise, the preparations for the conquest went forward. William received gifts and promises of men and ships; the old

166   The building of William's fleet (Bayeux tapestry)

167 A carpenter   168 William's sappers

Viking spirit of adventure came into play again, and the signs were auspicious.

Now while these things were doing, a great star appeared, shining for fourteen days, with three long rays streaming towards the south; such a star as is wont to be seen when a kingdom is about to change its king. [There was great enthusiasm. William] got together carpenters, smiths, and other workmen, so that great stir was seen at all the ports of Normandy, in the collecting of wood and materials, cutting of planks, framing of ships and boats, stretching sails and rearing masts, with great pains and at great cost. They spent all one summer and autumn in fitting up the fleet and collecting the forces.

Then the time came when they were ready to sail, and

they prayed the convent to bring out the shrine of S. Valeri, and set it on a carpet in the plain; and all came praying the holy reliques, that they might be allowed to pass over sea. They offered so much money, that the reliques were buried beneath it; and from that day forth, they had good weather and a fair wind.

Wace tells how

I heard my father say—I remember it well, although I was but a lad—that there were seven hundred ships, less four, when they sailed from S. Valeri; and that there were besides these ships, boats and skiffs for the purpose of carrying the arms and harness. [And when at length they started] The Duke placed a lantern on the mast of his ship, that the other ships might see it, and hold their course after it.

When they reached England,

169   William's army cooks

As the ships were drawn to shore, and the Duke first landed, he fell by chance upon his two hands. Forthwith all raised a loud cry of distress, "an evil sign," said they, "is here." But he cried out lustily, "See, seignors, by the splendour of God! I have seized England with my two hands; without challenge no prize can be made; all is our own that is here; and now we shall see who is the bolder man."

The archers

touched the land foremost, each with his bow bent and his quiver full of arrows slung at his side. All were shaven and shorn, and all clad in short garments, ready to attack, to shoot, to wheel about and skirmish. The knights landed next, all armed; with their hauberks on, their shields slung at their necks, and their helmets laced. They formed together on the shore, each armed upon his warhorse. All had their swords girded on, and passed into the plain with their lances raised. The barons had gonfanons, and the knights pennons. They occupied the advanced ground, next to where the archers had fixed themselves. The carpenters, who came after, had great axes in the hands, and planes and adzes at their sides. When they had reached the spot where the archers stood, and the knights were assembled, they consulted together, and sought for a good spot to place a strong fort upon. Then they cast out of the ships the materials and drew them to land, all shaped, framed and pierced to receive the pins which they had brought, cut and ready in large barrels; so that before evening had well set in, they had finished a fort. [Later a knight describes how] he saw them build up and enclose a fort, and dig the fosse around

170   William's army cooks

206

it [and] they strengthened it round about with palisades and a fosse.

The castle which Wace describes is similar to that shown on the Bayeux tapestry, which we illustrate in fig. *171*. It is called now the motte-and-bailey type. The motte was formed by scarping down a natural hill, or raising an artificial one with the earth dug out of the ditches. On this the fort was built and surrounded by a timber palisade. The ditch of the motte also encircled the bailey, and here were the stables, barns, kitchens, and barracks. The site always included a good spring of water. In such a castle William could leave a garrison to hold down the countryside. The Saxons had nothing so scientific at their disposal. Just as the Viking, with his ship as a base and his horse to carry him about, could deliver a blow at his own time, so the Normans, in the security of their castles, could select the moment for attack.

William knew all about building stone castles. Wace tells us how William of Arques built a tower above Arches (Chateau d'Arques, near Dieppe), and was besieged there by Duke William. The King of France came to the assistance of William of Arques, and Duke William, hearing of his intention, "strengthened his castles, cleaning the fosses, and repairing the walls. . . . Caen was then without a castle, and had neither wall nor fence to protect it". Stone walls are evidently meant here and differentiated from wooden fences or palisades. William built timber castles at first in England because they could be constructed quickly.

We can now return to the details of the Conquest and as the pages of Wace are read one becomes very sorry for the Saxons; they were beaten by the most wonderful staff work. William not only brought over castles packed in casks, but remembered that armies march on their stomachs. Wace tells how

> you might see them make their kitchens, light their fires, and cook their meat. The duke sat down to eat, and the barons and knights had food in plenty; for he had brought ample store. All ate and drank enough, and were right glad that they were ashore.

The Bayeux tapestry shows the Normans arriving at Pevensey, but according to Wace they first landed near Hastings and William "ordered proclamation to be made, and commanded

171 Motte-and-Bailey Castle

the sailors that the ships should be dismantled, and drawn ashore and pierced, that the cowards might not have the ships to flee to". This can only be regarded as a gesture to his men that they must do or die. William would hardly have cut off his line of retreat, or have built a fort at Hastings, except to leave a garrison in it to safeguard the fleet.

His next step was to move west about 12 miles to Pevensey. "The English were to be seen fleeing before them, driving off their cattle, and quitting their houses. All took shelter in the cemeteries, and even there they were in grievous alarm." Here again is evidence of staff work. Pevensey was one of the forts built about A.D. 300 by the Romans to protect the east and south coasts from the Saxon raids (*see* page 112). As the Roman walls with their bastions enclosing several acres are still standing today, they must, in William's time, have formed a good strong base where he could be safe and so compel Harold to come to him.

This was what poor Harold had to do. He came post haste from the Humber, from his encounter with Tosti, first to London, and then south again, and "erected his standard and fixed his gonfalon right where the Abbey of the Battle is now built", about 9 miles away from William at Pevensey. Here Harold dug himself in. "He had the place well examined and surrounded it by a good fosse, leaving an entrance on each of the three sides, which were ordered to be all well guarded."

We shall not concern ourselves very much with the details of the fighting, but there is one very interesting detail which must be noted. In the old Viking days, and the tale of Burnt Njal, fighting is mentioned quite casually, as fishing might be, or hunting. It was undertaken as a sport. From the time of the Normans onwards people sought to justify themselves. There were many parleys in 1066, and much talk of the justice of the respective causes. Each side appealed for the favour of Heaven, and there were threats of the dire consequences which would befall the opponent. The combatants, like modern boxers, reassured themselves and their backers, and appear to have stood in'need of support. When William

> prepared to arm himself, he called first for his good hauberk, and a man brought it on his arm and placed it before him; but in putting his head in to get it on, he inadvertently turned it the wrong

way, with the back part in front. He quickly changed it, but when he saw that those who stood by were sorely alarmed, he said, "I have seen many a man who, if such a thing happened to him, would not have borne arms or entered the field the same day; but I never believed in omens, and I never will. I trust in God."

One of Harold's spies, who had seen the Normans, reported that they "were so close shaven and cropt, that they had not even moustaches, supposed he had seen priests and mass-sayers; and he told Harold that the duke had more priests with him than knights or other people". But Harold replied, "Those are valiant knights, bold and brave warriors, though they bear not beards or moustaches as we do." William's priests were quite prepared to be useful. "Odo, the good priest, the bishop of Bayeux, 'was always found' where the battle was most fierce, and was of great service on that day."

After the battle, "The English who escaped from the field did not stop till they reached London." Again there is evidence of wonderful staff work. William did not at once pursue the enemy, but turned his attention to consolidating his position.

If our readers refer to the map (*I*), or the much better one of Roman Britain published by the Ordnance Survey, it will be seen why William selected Hastings as his point of attack. Pevensey was close by, all by itself and so more vulnerable. On the other hand, the usual entrance into England, by Watling Street, was protected by a group of forts at Lympne, Folkestone, Dover, Richborough, and Reculver. Some of these must have been in repair, because we read in Wace of how William went back east to Romney, which he destroyed, and then on to Dover. Obviously some Norman troops had been detailed to hold the English in check, and prevent them coming to the assistance of Harold, because Wace says that William did not rest "till he reached Dover, at the strong fort he had ordered to be made at the foot of the hill". Here he besieged the old Roman fort, and though the place was well fortified, took it after an eight-day siege. William placed a garrison in it, and was now ready for the great adventure; he had won a great battle; could he hold the country?

Canterbury rendered homage and delivered hostages to the Conqueror, who then journeyed to London. Arrived at Southwark, the citizens issued out of the gates, but were speedily

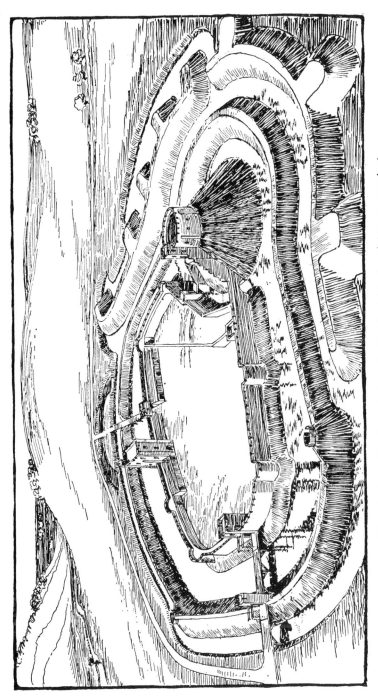

172   Air view of Berkhamsted Castle, Hertfordshire (partial reconstruction)

driven back, and the Normans burned all the houses on the south side of the Thames. Here again William gave another proof of genius. He had given the Londoners a taste of his quality, and his most urgent need was to thrust a spearhead in between his enemies before they had the opportunity to gather their forces together. This William did by going to Wallingford on the Thames, where it is thought that he crossed, and then passed by Icknield Way to the gap in the Chilterns at Tring, and then on to Berkhamsted. Again we will look at the map of Roman Britain and note that William's last raid gave him possession of many of the roads leading into London. First there was Stane Street from Portsmouth and Chichester. Then the very important road crossing the Thames at Staines, which branched off at Silchester into three roads serving the south and west. At Tring, William cut across Akeman Street, and could control Watling Street at Dunstable. The strategy was brilliantly successful, because the English surrendered and William received the crown of England in the grounds of Berkhamsted Castle.

We can now pass on to the work of the Normans when they were established in the country, and fig. *172* shows a reconstruction of Berkhamsted Castle. It is supposed that the earthworks and the mount are the work of Robert, Count of Mortain, who was in possession of Berkhamsted at the time of Domesday. Little remains now except earthworks and broken walls to mark an historic site, one which has seen perhaps as much of both the gay and the busy side of mediaeval life as any of our more ancient castles except Windsor. Thomas Becket was in charge of the works from 1155 to 1165. Edward III and the Black Prince held their courts within its walls. Froissart was another inhabitant, and Geoffrey Chaucer another clerk of the works. In 1930 this sadly neglected relic was placed under the guardianship of the Ministry of Works and put into a state of preservation.

The plan is of great interest because it shows the development of what is called the shell keep. As the artificial mottes became consolidated, the timber forts(*171*) were replaced with a stone wall. At Berkhamsted(*172*), when the mottes was excavated, it was discovered that this shell was about 60 feet external diameter, the wall being 8 feet thick. There would have been a

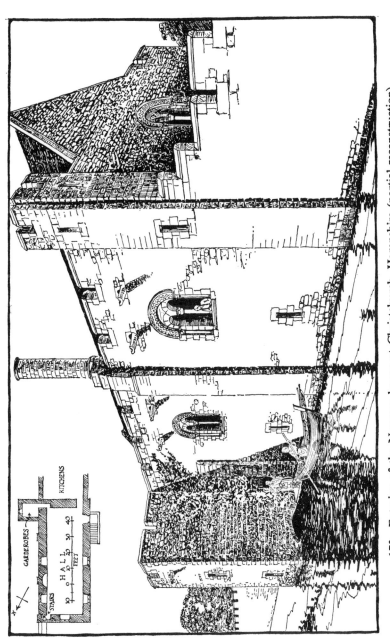

173 Exterior of the Norman house at Christchurch, Hampshire (partial reconstruction)

GARDEROBES

KITCHENS

STAIRS

H A L L

FEET

0 10 20 30 40

rampart walk on the top of this, and various sheds around it inside. There were steps up the motte, and these were protected by a tower at the top, and by the moat or ditch being taken around the motte at the base. The bailey had an inner and outer ward, and these were surrounded by flint rubble walls about 7 feet thick, of which some few parts remain. These had bastions and gates as shown, and were further protected by the two ditches and bank between, which make the castle so interesting.

The next development of the castle is shown in Volume I of *Everyday Things in England.*

We will now describe one of the most interesting buildings in England, the Norman House at Christchurch, Hampshire, the ruins of which are situated in the garden of the King's Head Hotel. The important detail to remember is that the English house started its life as a hall. On page 136 we have given a description of the hall in Beowulf, but here at Christchurch we can leave literary evidence behind, and look at the actual stones of an early twelfth-century house. It started life as the hall of the castle, and was built between 1125 and 1150. In Beowulf the hall is obviously on the ground floor level, but at Christchurch it has been moved to the first floor. This gave more sense of security, and enabled the windows to be bigger than would have been possible on the level of the ground. These had no glass, only wooden shutters for use at night. The hall was to remain on the first floor until life became a little more secure, in the fourteenth century, when it was moved downstairs, as at Penshurst.

Unfortunately the very considerable remains at Christchurch are so swathed with ivy that the walls are not only being destroyed, but it is very difficult to form any idea of what the building used to look like. However we have made a careful survey of the ruins, and figs. *173* and *174* are our reconstructions. The plan is very simple, just one large hall on the first floor, where the family lived, ate, and slept, because there was nowhere else to go. One remarkable detail is that there is a good fireplace in the hall, yet, side by side, the old custom of the fire in the centre of the hall was to remain till as late as 1570 at the Middle Temple Hall. At Christchurch the kitchens came at the south

174 The hall of the Norman house at Christchurch (partial reconstruction)

end of the hall, where also were the garderobes or latrines. At
the north end was a circular staircase, which led up to the
ramparts and down to a large room on the level of the ground,
where doubtless men-at-arms and stores were. Then, of course,
there would have been many sheds, stables, and barns, in the
castle bailey, which was surrounded by a wall. The house was
built as part of this wall, so that the inhabitants could look
across the mill stream, to which access was gained by a water
gate(*173*). The development of the house plan is shown in
Volume I of *Everyday Things in England*, where it can be seen
how other rooms were gradually grouped around the hall,
until, in the fifteenth century, the hall had become a house as
we understand it.

Backs of the king and queen   The knight

175–8 Chessmen found at Uig, Isle of Lewis, carved in morse ivory.
Twelfth century (*British Museum*)

Figs. *175–8* are of a magnificent set of chessmen now in the
British Museum. They are carved in morse ivory and were
found at Uig in the Isle of Lewis. They date from the twelfth
century. The people in the hall at Christchurch may have played
chess with chessmen like these. The king stands 4 inches high.
The warders, one biting his shield in rage, which take the place
of the castles, should be noted.

Now we are approaching the end of our task, and with superb
artistry have kept the really triumphant achievement of the
Normans for our finale! Unless we are careful, we look back

216

and think only of their castles; we may have been to the Tower of London, or have caught sight of Rochester on our way along that very old way, Watling Street, or we may have been to Castle Hedingham, Essex. These three wonderful keeps may have oppressed our spirits, as they did the Saxons who were held

179 The interior of Hemel Hempstead Church, Hertfordshire
(partial reconstruction)

217

in thrall under their walls. Stare, stark, and strong, these great walls rear themselves up, yet they are full of delightful little bits of detail which gladden the architect. Judged only by their castles, the Normans would seem too fierce and formidable, but when we come to their cathedrals and churches, there is a very different tale to tell. The architecture is still fierce and proud. It lacks the grace of the thirteenth century, and makes you think of a race of priests who could challenge kings and usurers. Abbot Samson, of whom Carlyle wrote in *Past and Present*, and Becket were of the same breed—turbulent, but very strong, and not given to compromise or half measures in their fight against evil. There is hardly a cathedral in England in which their hand cannot be traced, and their vision and grasp of planning was superb; it was almost as if they took William's favourite oath as their motto and built to the "Splendour of God". The zenith of the architectural achievement of the Normans can be seen at Durham, where the great Norman cathedral is one of the most impressive churches of its period in Western Europe.

We have selected for our illustrations, not a cathedral, but the church of Hemel Hempstead, Hertfordshire, which shows how the Normans went to work when they wanted to build a parish church in a small market town about 1140.

The plan(*181*) shows that the men of Hemel Hempstead, in 1140, understood the value of a simple layout of cruciform type, and fig. *179* how this resolved itself into a wonderful interior, in which one looked through darkness into light. Fig. *180* is the exterior. Our illustrations have been made from sketches of the actual building, and the few liberties we have taken have only been in the way of eliminating later work and restoring the Norman detail: internally, we have omitted the modern "Gothic" choir stalls, and externally the later leaded spire is not shown on the Norman tower, and so on. The church has, fortunately for us, escaped the vandalism of the nineteenth century in a surprising fashion.

Fig. *182* shows the vaulting to the chancel, and is an amusing example of how the old masons played with the problems of solid geometry. The Normans at first used the plain semicircular barrel vault. Then one day somebody made two of these vaults cross as A(*182*), but the result did not satisfy them for long, because the intersections, or groins, at B, were necessarily

218

180 Exterior of Hemel Hempstead Church (partial reconstruction)

THE COMING OF THE NORMANS

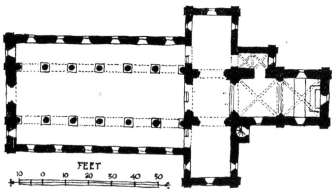

181   Plan of Hemel Hempstead Church

flatter than a semi-circle; they had to be, because their span was greater than that of the vault, and they had to spring, and finish, at the same levels. So the next step was to make the groin itself semi-circular, as shown in the main drawing of fig. *182* at C. Then the cross ribs at D had to be raised up on legs, or stilted, to reach to the height of the groins. This was really a little clumsy, so the cross rib was turned into a pointed arch. But that is another story which is told in Volume I of *Everyday Things in England*, where we show how step by step the old masons progressed up to the glorious fan vaulting of Henry the VII's Chapel at Westminster Abbey.

182   Chancel vaulting, Hemel Hempstead Church

If this church at Hemel Hempstead is compared with those of the Anglo-Saxons we have illustrated, it will be noted how great an advance the Normans made in the art of building; there is no fumbling with their work, but a splendid self-confidence. They were a wonderful people and their stock first comes into notice with the Norsemen, or Northmen, who raided our

220

land as Vikings. We must bear in mind their travels to the East through Russia, their discoveries by land, and their adventures by sea. They were a people, and it is a period, to which far more detailed study should be given than is possible in this little book.

England has welcomed many men. The man of the Old Stone Age; the Mediterranean men of the New Stone Age; and the Celts. Rome and her legionaries brought blood from all over Europe. Then came the Angles, Saxons, and Jutes; the Vikings and Normans; the Angevins, Flemings, Huguenots, and all the other races who have drifted in. Age after age the soil of our island has attracted men; here they have lived and, dying, their bones or ashes have been turned into the soil of England. Each in their turn have made their contribution to the common stock, and the genius of the race, and the Viking, Norseman, or Norman, was not the least of these men. It may well be that England will go forward just so long as their courage and love of adventure are not allowed to be swamped by the vulgar chaffering of the market place.

CHRONOLOGY

THE ROMAN OCCUPATION OF BRITAIN

B.C.

55   CAESAR makes a reconnaissance and returns to Gaul.

54   CAESAR invades in force: marches into Kent, defeats CASSIVEL-LAUNUS, and once more retires to Gaul.

      CAESAR's attempt to conquer Britain has failed. Celtic chieftains again hold undisputed sway.

A.D.

43   CLAUDIUS invades. His expeditionary force, under AULUS PLAUTIUS, lands at Richborough. CARACTACUS and TOGO-DUMNUS are defeated on the Medway. Verulam becomes a *municipium*. CLAUDIUS occupies Colchester. The legions push slowly northwards and westwards, the future Emperor VESPASIAN commanding the Second Legion.

47   P. OSTORIUS SCAPULA succeeds PLAUTIUS as Governor. He creates a frontier on the Fosse Way. He moves against CARAC-TACUS, now military leader of the Silures of South Wales.

51   OSTORIUS defeats CARACTACUS, who flees to CARTIMAN-DUA, Queen of the Brigantes, and is betrayed by her to the Romans. He ends his days as a prisoner at Rome.

53   The Silures fight on. OSTORIUS dies, worn out by his exertions, and is succeeded by the unenterprising DIDIUS GALLUS.

58   The enterprising D. VERANIUS NEPOS sets out to cow the Silures, but dies within the year.

59   C. SUETONIUS PAULINUS, an able and ruthless general, becomes Governor and marches into Wales.

61   PAULINUS reaches the Menai Straits. He invades Anglesey, last refuge of the Druids, and puts them to the sword. But BOUDICCA (BOADICEA), Queen of the Iceni, has revolted in far-off Norfolk. While PAULINUS races back with his cavalry, she sacks Colchester and annihilates the Ninth Legion. Then she destroys Verulam and London, nearly succeeding in driving the Romans from Britain. PAULINUS wins a brilliant victory against superior numbers. BOUDICCA takes poison. Reprisals of the utmost severity follow the revolt. The Procurator, JULIUS CLASSICIANUS, protests against PAULINUS' inhumanity. The Emperor NERO replaces PAULINUS by C. PETRONIUS TURPILIANUS.

63   TREBELLIUS MAXIMUS becomes Governor. Comparative peace in Britain.

71   The Brigantes become restless. The harsh PETILLIUS CERIALIS is sent by VESPASIAN to subdue them.

CHRONOLOGY

74 The determined SEXTUS JULIUS FRONTINUS is made Governor He succeeds in the task of suppressing the Welsh tribes.

78 GNAEUS JULIUS AGRICOLA, third of VESPASIAN's fighting Governors, extinguishes the last sparks of Welsh and Brigantian resistance.

81 AGRICOLA makes himself master of Scotland, as far as the Forth and Clyde.

83 AGRICOLA thrusts into the Highlands and beats the massed Caledonian armies at Mons Graupius, a celebrated encounter.

84 The Emperor DOMITIAN, preoccupied with his German campaigns, recalls AGRICOLA at the victorious climax of his Governorship, AGRICOLA leaves Britain an embittered man.
Records are scanty for British military history in the latter part of the reign of DOMITIAN and in the reign of TRAJAN.
Names of Governors preserved in inscriptions are:
SALLUSTIUS LUCULLUS.
NEPOS.

98 T. AVIDIUS QUIETUS.

103 L. NERIATUS MARCELLUS.
Reign of HADRIAN begins.
Q. POMPEIUS FALCO.

121 The Emperor HADRIAN visits Britain.

122 A. PLATORIUS NEPOS, an intimate friend of the Emperor, constructs Hadrian's Wall between 122–126-7.

130 JULIUS SEVERUS becomes Governor.

140 Q. LOLLIUS URBICUS, the next Governor, campaigns in Scotland. He builds the Antonine Wall, of turf, across the Forth–Clyde isthmus between 140–142-3.

155 The Brigantes revolt and are put down by C. JULIUS VERUS.

169 The Emperor MARCUS AURELIUS sends reinforcements to M. STATIUS PRISCUS, who has succeeded VERUS. Britain is again fanned by the flame of revolt.

180 At the beginning of the reign of the Emperor COMMODUS, the Caledonians burst through the Antonine Wall. It is at this point that the military initiative in Britain passes from the Romans to their enemies, with whom it remains to the end of the occupation.

184 The war in Britain ends. COMMODUS assumes the title BRITAN-NICUS to commemorate the victory, due to the efforts of the stern ULPIUS MARCELLUS.

185 HELVIUS PERTINAX succeeds MARCELLUS and puts down a mutiny in the Roman army in Britain.

193 COMMODUS is assassinated. The Praetorian Guard elects PER-TINAX Emperor, then turns on him and butchers him. There is civil war in Rome. SEPTIMIUS SEVERU8 seizes power. CLODIUS ALBINUS, successor of PERTINAX in Britain, proclaims himself Emperor and crosses with his troops to Gaul.

196 SEVERUS marches on Lyons, where ALBINUS has set up court. ALBINUS commits suicide. In consequence of the removal of the garrison by ALBINUS in his bid for the throne, the Barbarians over-run all N. England, wrecking Hadrian's Wall and dismantling the great fortresses at York and Chester.

198 SEVERUS sends VIRIUS LUPUS to Britain to repair the havoc wrought by the Barbarians. LUPUS, and after him ALFENUS SENECIO, reconstructs Hadrian's Wall between 198–208.

208 SEVERUS in person attacks the Caledonians. He penetrates nearly to the extreme northern tip of Britain.

211 Worn out by his arduous campaign in Scotland, SEVERUS dies at York. But his work of pacification in Britain is effective. Britain enjoys peace during the subsequent upheavals elsewhere in the Empire.

286 The Admiral of the British fleet, M. AURELIUS CARAUSIUS, sets up Britain as an independent empire. The two Augusti, DIOCLETIAN and MAXIMIAN, acknowledge the picturesque CARAUSIUS as one of themselves. In addition to Britain, he is allotted a strip of N. France.

293 DIOCLETIAN's general. CONSTANTIUS CHLORUS, is in-structed to seize CARAUSIUS' French possessions. Meanwhile CARAUSIUS is murdered by the contemptible ALLECTUS, his finance minister.

296 CONSTANTIUS crosses the Channel and defeats ALLECTUS, who is slain in battle. CONSTANTIUS, vigorous and popular, effects widespread reorganization in Britain.

306 CONSTANTIUS, after a protracted encounter with the Picts, dies at York. His son, known to history as CONSTANTINE THE GREAT, assumes the title of CAESAR IMPERATOR.

337 CONSTANS, son of CONSTANTINE, fights the Picts (from Scotland) and the Scots (from Ireland).

350 CONSTANS is murdered, MAGNUS MAGNENTIUS, the Gaulish usurper, is killed by CONSTANTIUS II, together with the beloved MATINUS, *vicarius* of Britain.

360 The cruel LUPICINUS is sent to Britain.

368 In the reign of VALENTINIAN I, a concerted attack is made on Britain, by Picts, Scots, Saxons, Franks, and Attacotti (a confedera-tion of tribes in Ireland). The Roman troops are everywhere routed. VALENTINIAN despatches the Spanish COUNT THEODOSIUS to clear the country of the barbarians, installed throughout the entire land. THEODOSIUS carries out the difficult mission successfully.

383 MAGNUS MAXIMUS denudes Britain of its garrison to seize the throne of the Empire from VALENTINIAN's son GRATIAN, who is murdered. Britain, left defenceless, once more succumbs to barbarian hordes. Hadrian's Wall makes its last defence.

393 STILICHO, regent in Britain of the Emperor THEODOSIUS, son of COUNT THEODOSIUS, once again liberates Britain.

CHRONOLOGY

399 STILICHO completes the war of liberation. He enlists the aid of CUNEDDA, a British chieftain, to help in the work of pacification.

401 STILICHO is forced to withdraw troops from Britain to help protect the Empire from the advancing Goths.

403 ALARIC the Goth is defeated at Verona. RADAGAISUS begins a fresh Gothic invasion.

405 The troops in Britain, in despair, set up successive usurpers called MARCUS, GRATIAN, and finally CONSTANTINE to provide for the defence of the country.

410 The Emperor HONORIUS tells the people of Britain that Rome is no longer in a position to come to their aid. STILICHO has been murdered, and ALARIC is marching on Rome. HONORIUS' rescript marks the end of the Roman occupation of Britain, though at the time both Rome and Britain believed that their fortunes would sooner or later be reunited.

430 By this date the government of Britain is being decisively taken over by the Saxons.

446 The British make a last appeal to AETIUS. The appeal is rejected. The bond with Rome is completely sundered.

ANGLO-SAXON, VIKING, AND NORMAN TIMES

A.D.
313 Roman toleration of Christianity.
410 Roman protection withdrawn.
410–c. 520 Settlement of England by Saxons.
c. 432 St. Patrick goes to Ireland.
467–93 The legend of Arthur may rest on a British king who resisted the Saxon invaders at this time.
519 CERDIC and CYNRIC (kings of West Saxons).
520 Britons win battle at Mount Bedon.
545–6 *De Excidio*—Gildas.
547 IDA, King of Bernicia.
552 West Saxons take Old Sarum (near Salisbury).
560 ÆTHELBERT, King of Kent, *d.* 616.
c. 563 St. Columba goes to Iona.
568 Æthelbert defeated by West Saxons.
c. 570 Birth of Mahomet at Mecca.
571 West Saxons invade Mid-Britain.
577 West Saxons win battle at Deorham.
584 West Saxons defeated at Faddiley.
588 ÆTHELRIC, King of Northumbria.
593 ÆTHELFRITH, King of Northumbria, *d.* 617.
597 Landing of Augustine. He restores St. Martin's Church at Canterbury.

603 Battle of Daegsasten.
613 Battle of Chester.
617 EADWINE, King of Northumbria. *d.* 633.
625 Conversion of Eadwine. Paulinus converts Northumbria.
626 PENDA, King of Mercians, *d.* 655.
626 Supremacy of Eadwine.
633 OSWALD, King of Bernicia. *d.* 641
633 Eadwine killed at Hatfield by Mercians.
633 Defeat of Welsh by Oswald.
635 Aidan goes to Holy Island.
c. 640 Conversion of Wessex.
650–60 Sutton Hoo Ship Burial.
654 OSWIU, King of Northumbria. *d.* 670.
655 Battle at Winwaed.
658 West Saxons invade to the Parret.
659 WULFHERE, King of Mercia.
661 West Saxons retreat across the Thames.
664 Council of Whitby. Caedmon at Whitby.
668 Theodore of Tarsus, Archbishop of Canterbury.
670 ECGFRITH, King of Northumbria. *d.* 685.
670–80 Brixworth Church, Northants. Wing Church, Bucks. St. Pancras Church, Canterbury. Bewcastle and Ruthwell Crosses.
673 Birth of Bede.
675 ÆTHELRED, King of Mercia. *d.* 704.
681 Completion of English conversion. South Saxons embrace Christianity under Wilfrid; heathen burials cease.
681 Crypt at Hexham built.
681 The Lindisfarne Gospels.
682 Escomb Church, Durham.
687 Death of St. Cuthbert.
688 INE, King of West Saxons, *d.* 726.
688 Conquest of Mid-Somerset by Wessex.
c. 700 Franks Casket (Northumbria).
715 Bradford-on-Avon Church.
716 ÆTHELBALD, King of Mercia, *d.* 757.
716 Defeat of Mercia by West Saxons.
c. 730 Bede, the first English historian, writes his Ecclesiastical History.
733 Mercia conquers Wessex.
735 Death of Bede.
753 Death of Boniface.
754 Wessex wins Battle of Burford.
757 OFFA, King of Mercia. *d.* 796.
775 Mercia subdues Kent.
792 Sack of Lindisfarne by the Vikings.
793 Foundation of St. Albans Monastery.
796 COENWULF, King of Mercia. *d.* 821.
c. 800 Historia Brittorium (Nennius).
802 ECGBERHT, King of Wessex. *d.* 839.

CHRONOLOGY

815   Final conquest of British.
828   Supremacy of Ecgberht.
837   Defeat of Danes by Ecgberht.
839   ÆTHELWULF, King of Wessex. *d.* 858.
849   Birth of Ælfred.
851   Defeat of Danes at Aclea.
857   ÆTHELBALD, King of Wessex, *d.* 860.
860   ÆTHELBERT, King of Wessex. *d.* 866.
866   Danes land in East Anglia.
867   Danes conquer Northumbria and capture York.
867   St. Michael's Church, St. Albans.
c. 868   Martyrdom of Eadmund.
871   ÆLFRED, King of Wessex, *d.* 899.
871   Danes invade East Anglia and Wessex.
878   Ælfred wins battle at Edington—Peace of Wedmore.
891-2   Start of compilation of Anglo-Saxon Chronicle.
897   Ælfred builds a Fleet.
899   EADWARD THE ELDER, *d.* 925.
912   Northmen attack Normandy.
912   Deerhurst Church, Glos.
925   ÆTHELSTAN, *d.* 939.
939   EADMUND, *d.* 946.
943   Dunstan, Abbot of Glastonbury.
946   EADRED, *d.* 955.
954   Submission of Danelaw—England becomes one kingdom.
955   EADWIG, *d.* 959.
958   EADGAR, *d.* 975.
959   Dunstan, Archbishop of Canterbury.
975   EADWARD THE MARTYR, *d.* 979.
978   ÆTHELRED THE UNREADY, *d.* 1016.
978   Benedictine rule introduced.
978   Worth Church, Sussex.
991   Vikings defeat East Anglians at Maldon.
991   Barnack Church, Northants.
1013   England submits to Swein.
1016   EADMUND IRONSIDE, *d.* 1016.
1016   CNUT, *d.* 1035.
1016   Breamore Church, Hants.
1027   Birth of William of Normandy.
1037   HARALD, *d.* 1040.
1037   Earls Barton Church, Northants.
1042   EADWARD THE CONFESSOR., *d.* 1066.
1051   Bosham Church, Sussex.
1054-6   Normans conquer Southern Italy.
1060   Normans invade Sicily.
1060-80   Close of paganism in Scandinavia.
1066   HAROLD.

CHRONOLOGY

1066   Harold defeats Hardrada at Stamford Bridge and is defeated himself at Senlac.
1066   WILLIAM THE CONQUEROR.
1070   Lanfranc, Archbishop of Canterbury, reorganizes Church.
c. 1080   St. Benet Church, Cambridge. Sompting Church, Sussex.
1086   Domesday Book completed.

INDEX

The numerals in **heavy type** refer to the **figure numbers** of the illustrations

INDEX

INDEX

233

INDEX